GARDENING WITH KIDS

GARDENING

WITH KIDS

by

Sharon MacLatchie

® Rodale Press, Emmaus, PA

Printed in the United States of America on recycled paper

Library of Congress Cataloging in Publication Data

MacLatchie, Sharon.
Gardening with kids.

Bibliography: p.
Includes index.
1. Children's gardens. 2. Organic gardening.
I. Title.
SB457.M3 635'.02'4054 77-24215
ISBN 0-87857-171-X

2 4 6 8 10 9 7 5 3

Dedication

To John, Johnny and Danielle,
who made it possible

Contents

Acknowledgments

I am grateful to the following friends for their valuable contributions to this book: Duane Newcomb for his help in making the idea a reality and sharing material; Frank LaMoglia for his photographic skill; Dennis Stewart for research and advice; Helmer Felton for sharing his experiences gardening with groups; Sheryl Harris for introducing me to organic gardening; Glenn G. Vincent of Park Seed Company for information on minivegetables; Allan A. Swenson for help on rare plants; Betty Wisham for material and encouragement; Bill Hylton for ideas and enthusiasm from the beginning; and to those too numerous to mention who shared experiences.

Introduction

Parents garden with their children for many reasons. Among them, gardening is a fun, worthwhile and inexpensive way to spend time together.

In our case, we began gardening with our two-year-old son, not with lofty thoughts of parent-child relationships, the joys of working together and sharing precious moments—what we call "superparent" reasons. These we experienced, to be sure, but much later.

No, in the beginning, gardening seemed the perfect solution to the troubles we, as new parents, were experiencing. We could *dig* out our frustrations in the garden instead of tearing our hair out, and have vegetables as an added bonus. A simple enough system which worked pretty well, until our son, Johnny, began to walk.

Looking back on that first year in our garden, we had an extraordinary amount of luck. Our squash plants produced abundantly, enough to supply our small family and much of the neighborhood. Our tomatoes were the epitome of health, putting forth prodigious quantities of lush, juicy, simply delicious fruit. Even the old apricot tree redoubled its efforts on our behalf; I learned to can and store fruit for winter. The strawberries, however, were another story.

We had planted five end-of-the-season bargains two years before, as groundcover more than anything else. Whatever we did, our berries flourished and promised to bear heavily in June. Our good fortune didn't last. Not snails or slugs or poor weather, but another surreptitious villain who decided strawberries had strained baby fruits beat hands down.

We caught our son a couple of days later with the evidence smeared from earlobes to knees. So ended the mystery and began our vigilante action—after all, strawberries in copious quantities give little boys stomach aches.

We fenced the entire garden next weekend. It worked well for two weeks. Then our son learned to squeeze by, greatly reducing the life expectancy of our newly transplanted seedlings. The strawberries continued to disappear at an alarming rate, and with them, our dreams of a year-long supply of homemade strawberry jam stored next to the apricots. We despaired of ever having a garden, when the truth dawned—maybe we were taking the wrong approach.

For one thing, as our beginner's luck yielded pounds of fresh vegetables through the summer, Johnny would try virtually anything we picked and handed him—much more than we could say for the attractively packaged baby foods sitting on our kitchen shelves. And he really enjoyed squatting to examine a little plant with one forefinger. Plants, it seems, unlike most of his childhood world, were just the right size. The actual damage, once we assessed it, wasn't all that bad. The number of stomach aches subsided, then shrank to nought as we handed out the strawberries each evening. Finally we agreed if he could figure out on his own how to wriggle by the fence, maybe we could teach him where to step and where not to.

It was thus we started to include him. He's learned so much in a short time. Our son, just four, can lead his preschool class through the garden, naming the vegetables and pointing out those that are ripe. And our daughter, Danielle, just over one year, won't be far behind.

Believe me, we've learned too—not only how to survive in a garden with children, but how to enjoy them and gardening as well. It's taken a great amount of adjustment in our thinking, for sure. Gardening successfully with children takes a whole new approach and a bit of imagination. Several years down the road, we've thankfully left behind the negative reasons for including our children and have discovered the terrific benefits we and our children experience by gardening together. I have no doubt you can too.

If the idea of gardening with your children turns you on, then this is the book for you. Even if you're an inexperienced gardener, as we were, you and your child can quickly learn successful organic gardening. But why *organic* gardening?

There are certainly many arguments for going strictly organic today, one of the most practical and adult being economic. In general, materials used in organic soil building are readily available and very often free. A better argument, one germane to gardening with children, is that kids and chemicals simply don't mix safely. No one needs to quote statistics on child poisonings each year—as parents we're only too well aware. The fewer potentially harmful materials we keep around the home, the better our chances of preventing a hapless accident, particularly when working with young children.

The child today who can learn to raise his food without petroleum-based chemical fertilizers will find his skill valuable, maybe *vital* to his future survival. Other sound reasons are closely tied to children's psychology, as we'll discuss later—your child's need for independence, which certainly is in tune with finding resources for food growing within Nature and labor-intensive methods; and the need for a good relationship with the environment, forefront in the minds of children who are very ecologically aware. Finally, there is challenge. The degree of satisfaction gained from growing food and other plants without having to resort to "artificial" means is intense, as witnessed by the tremendous growth in popularity of organic gardening in the past five years.

As anyone who has worked with children in any project knows, experience and preplanning are vital to success. If you're inexperienced in organic gardening, remember that with children to minimize failure is keynote. Success works miracles in youthful psyches and isn't bad for grownups either. After initial preparation you'll learn the basics along with your child. The techniques and activities described are chosen with children's expectations in mind and are specifically recommended because of their appeal to children.

Each chapter, whether about how to get started with summer vegetables, how to beat the bugs, or how to garden indoors, offers every child something he can do. Your preschooler will be able to handle much from start to finish with your help. Older children, once they've learned the basics, may expand their skills toward complete food growing, competition growing, even gardening for income. Together, you can aim for success early and repeatedly with skills you'll both learn.

If you're an experienced organic gardener, your knowledge can be used to great advantage. Success in gardening with children depends largely on thinking in their terms—thus the challenge. As an experienced organic gardener, you can show your child day-to-day dynamics of the garden patch when your child thinks nothing is happening. You can help expand his interest beyond the ordinary to the special, maybe toward a lifelong hobby.

Whatever your gardening skill, begin first by remembering how a child experiences the world, then participate with him.

CHAPTER 1

Silver Bells and Cockleshells

Why Garden with Children?

A good question and one which, when answered, leads us right to the other important question. What's the best way to approach organic gardening with your child?

Down the Rabbit Hole

Any adult who spends even fifteen minutes with a child outdoors finds himself drawn back to his own childhood, like Alice falling down the rabbit hole. When our child discovers a tree frog, butterflies or the first lettuce seeds sprouting, our own childhood memories of spring's freshness, fall's windy excitement, even certain smells, rush upon us and for a few moments we've remembered—even become—kids again.

But better than memories is promise. Our children in their inexperience can lead us to think again about what we take for granted. There is always something new happening in the garden. On our hands and knees we peer into a crevice or curled leaf searching out a culprit. We get an entirely different perspective when we look up. Eye-level with our child, the world looks enormous. When we try to figure out what caused a calamity in our garden, it's refreshing to know that as adults, we haven't experienced it all. There are still discoveries to be made. Gardening with our children can lead us there.

Our children will question what we simply accept. How

There are still discoveries to be made.

come you just pulled up that plant when it took so long to grow? Why do plants have to die? Why do seeds grow when you put them in the ground? How does that seed know it's supposed to be a tree when it grows up? Penetrating questions, and enough to tax the skill of any parent faced with giving simple answers.

Where Do Things Come From?

It's an unfortunate fact of modern life that children who are brought up in urban areas experience very little of what could be termed "the basics" before their school years. The supermarket with its rows of milk cartons, topless cold-storage carrots and dried potato flakes is inadequate as an explanation of where food comes from, let alone a help in understanding life. Gardening can be.

The garden *is* a physical life cycle, and when we garden with our children we draw them into it. Vital experiences are there in meaningful form—beginnings, life, nurturing, calamity, death. When you garden with your children, you lay the groundwork for later understanding of human life and experiences.

But unless curiosity is fostered and given opportunity to expand, his natural curiosity will fade as skills are mastered if your child is not guided in new directions.

A parent who gardens with his child from the earliest years does much to sustain that curiosity. But no matter how many opportunities you can dream up, it should be remembered that children by and large are not self-starters. Which means your participation—digging, planting and harvesting right along with your child—is all important. Gardening *with* your child adds a new dimension to his or her learning. It leads to success in a way merely giving directions can't.

Children may not be self-starters, but I know ours don't want to be told, either. Children work best when they are in on the action, but allowed to make discoveries themselves.

Providing opportunities for discovery is one of the surest ways to stimulate and sustain your child's natural curiosity.

Enjoyment Above All

Ever notice how the time demands of jobs, households and social obligations extract more and more of our time until it seems we scarcely manage our children's physical needs, let alone the "extras" like really listening to them and just having fun together?

Gardening has distinct advantages for busy parents who want more time with their children. It is usually home based, which means that whatever else is necessary for their care is available too—a real plus for the family with young children.

Gardening isn't fast. It's planning, planting, waiting, tending, harvesting and preparation for eating. There's time for discussion, water fights and lemonade. As such, it can be enjoyed at odd moments when other obligations are taken care of. In most instances gardening can be picked up and left with a minimum of problem. And there is no expedition to prepare for. What's more, gardening is outdoors. When much of our work is indoors, taking the kids for a stint outside can be pure bliss.

The range of recreational activities available to the average family today is limited only by their ambitions and, unfortunately, their financial situation. Gardening with the children, unlike trips to Disneyland or weekly sessions at a local movie theater, usually pays back several-fold any amount initially invested. Few enjoyable "recreations" can offer that!

Gardening isn't just play, either—it's work too. While merely having fun has an important place in all our lives, raising our own food, even small amounts, is really doing something that has a tangible purpose. Like exercising our bodies (which gardening also does), the results are visible and impart a sense of worth and time well spent. With children, work and play are one and the same. Your children, like mine, will enjoy being productive.

Recreation or work, and it's both, the greatest benefit we as parents will derive from gardening with our children is pleasure—those pure and precious moments shared together.

What Your Child Will Expect

Remember what great things you expected as a child, especially when you were small? And how many things measured up? On the other hand, how many didn't?

No matter what your child's age, whatever you do together to help your gardening project measure up to his or her expectations will put you on the road to a worthwhile, enjoyable time. But can your garden meet your child's expectations, which for younger children are at best grandiose, for older children promising challenge? Well, the answer is yes and no. The difference, we've found, is how carefully you plan around what you hope to get and to what extent your child is actively included from the time you first begin leafing through seed catalogs.

Such planning is imperative. A garden can fail through lack of good soil preparation and layout, lack of care midseason, or simply ill-timed harvest. Failures of any kind in parent-child projects are psychological negatives, which we all wish to avoid. But forget about failures and concentrate on successful gardening with your child.

First of all, make your garden largely your *child's* garden right from the start. Second, keep in mind how your child looks at things, what he is learning as a maturing person, what he expects, and in that vein, how things in your gardening project are measuring up. Finally, aim for gardening success early and repeatedly.

For instance, we've found certain vegetables are better matched to small children. In general, quick germinating, hearty, easy care, large seeded, brightly colored vegetables that taste good are just right for small gardeners. Impossible to find? Not at all. Nature abounds with them as we'll see in chapter 3.

But just what do children expect anyhow? First of all surprise. Here's your opportunity to play detective and teacher rolled into one, by continually leading your child to "discover" the surprises in the garden—and every garden has them. Ours certainly does. There's a covey of thirty or more quail who found refuge under gigantic squash leaves. Cottontail rabbits who invade and threaten to demolish the lettuce patch. Then there are the perennial residents of the compost area—red "fishing" worms and a horrendous creature reminiscent of the dinosaur age, the Jerusalem cricket. About six inches in length with huge mandibles and long antennae, he'd impress the most nonchalant in your family. Then there are the gophers and king snakes, plus residents of all gardens—spiders, sow bugs, birds, squirrels and frogs. Our garden, yours too, is a haven for small- and medium-sized wildlife.

Which brings us to the second expectation of children—to participate in *everything*—digging, planting, choosing, harvesting and socializing with those fauna your lush patch has become a home for.

Personally, I'm not an insect fan. And to show you what damage an unthinking parent can do, I terrified my son so badly about spiders when he first toddled around the garden, that from then on he would stand petrified, pointing and crying any time one crossed his path. And if there was only one in the whole garden, be sure that he would find it. After that incident, I decided some rethinking was in order. Most of the "critters" in our garden are harmless, and quite frankly, caterpillars, ladybugs and sow bugs make more desirable playmates than some I can think of. My rule from then on has been: if they won't do them harm, let the kids play.

While your child should participate in everything, there is a limit to how much he or she will be able to do on his own.

As parents of young children, we expect to, and do, most of the physical work. Parents of older children can offer more by way of guidance, and probably less behind-the-shovel expertise.

Another big item on your child's expect-list will be doing things his way. And while you're in this together, there's *really* no reason why all things have to grow in straight rows, we found out. Be sure your child will ask, if he's not the superneat type, or more likely he'll just proceed to plant things where they suit him. If the conditions are right for an individual plant, let your child be creative.

What Your Child Will Learn

The wonder of life, an ongoing fascination with its mysteries, a search for further knowledge and pure enjoyment—all good reasons for parents to garden with their children. What about your child? What will he or she learn from your experiences together?

Much said thus far has been directed to parents of young families. But if your children are older, gardening with them offers special opportunities to help them grow.

I'm O.K., You're O.K.

The psychological needs of growing children have been studied and defined for many years. As parents, most of us know them intuitively.

First and above all, to feel they are worthwhile children must experience success. Today, when classes are divided into groups largely determined by reading ability, many children who don't excel academically can believe they're not measuring up to expectations.

Gardening provides so many opportunities for *every* child to learn and use other skills: *design*, by planning what goes where in relation to the sun and garden surroundings; *comparative*, by choosing good plant varieties for the area; *physical*, by muscling a garden tiller; *creative*, by making wire supports, trellises or greenhouses; and all around *green-thumb*, by producing a bountiful harvest. Every child can excel somewhere.

For the child who doesn't succeed in school to the point of recognition, any project he can plan and carry out successfully will add much to the way he feels about himself and his abilities. The school gardens springing up all over the country mean educators are finally saying it: academics aren't everything; the child who can learn to raise carrots has something to be proud of. If your child's confidence in himself needs a boost, gardening at home together can be the way.

Closely behind a child's need for success comes the need for reassurance. Children often feel at odds with their world and, consequently, uneasy. Nature, as any gardener knows, is completely impartial. The child whose tomato vines wither may be inclined to blame himself. Then he looks at his neighbor's and finds a like disaster has befallen hers. While the example is negative, the results are positive—your child will learn some things are just beyond human control; not everything is our fault.

Praise is probably the best reassurance you can offer your children. It is their guarantee that you're really interested in them, that you've taken the time to evaluate and appreciate what they have done.

Along with not feeling at odds with his or her surroundings, a maturing child should feel in tune with his surroundings—his personal ecology. How does your child begin to feel one with his surroundings? Above all, by working *with* Nature.

Research and current disaster have taught all of us the need for a harmonious relationship with the Earth. If your child is in school, chances are you hear as much about ecology as the dangers of smoking. Because you're choosing organic gardening methods, he'll be able to put his awareness into action. Turning a weedy corner of the yard into lush, edible vegetables means your child has cooperated with Nature to change indifference to beneficence, and that's a lot.

Children's need for independence from adults is probably never greater than it is today. Do you remember the first paycheck you ever earned? I do. Mine was for ten dollars, earned by eight hours of exhausting work. You probably remember, like me, staring long at that first check and thinking, I worked for this, it's mine. Whatever age, we'd come a long way from dependence on adults simply by proving to ourselves we could achieve on our own what we had set out to do.

Simply put, we are, as a group, able to give our children more materially than our parents could manage. Which means children today may have fewer ways to "earn" their independence. Fortunately, independence isn't limited to earning a living. Children can achieve gradual self-sufficiency in a number of ways. First, by accepting increasing responsibility.

The more you encourage your child to accept responsibility in your gardening project, the more you point the way toward his independence. Adolescents can become completely involved and assume responsibility for well-managed, year-round food production. Others, younger children, will be very interested in money-making side benefits like running a neighborhood lemonade stand or fruit stall. Whatever your child may pick as his special domain, your encouragement to total responsibility will help him become self-sufficient.

Notice though, the word, "encouragement." Encouraging your child in a joint growing venture is different from *ordering* him to do something. Orders presuppose submission and are a big turn-off. A small child's sense of responsibility can be jogged simply with, "Did you know vegetables need plenty of water to grow?" Older children are receptive to the plain facts of the situation—without watering and weeding, vegetables die.

Second, children become self-sufficient by proving to themselves they can accomplish what they set out to do. There is a temptation with children to turn to another project just when the first is getting under way. Like responsibility, your child needs encouragement toward persistence. Now is the time to rely on your child's curiosity and your parental imagination. Find out what's *really* going on in the garden, or add another related project like building a miniature greenhouse. We've found encouragement, not insistence, is what counts.

Closely aligned with the need for independence, children should learn about their future role as adults. Just what does being adult mean?

When gardening with your child, along with accepting responsibility, it means making decisions. In your garden there are many to be made, like what to plant, of which variety, when to plant it, where and how much. What to fertilize with, which pest control method to use—hand, biological or both, are other decisions which must be made as your garden progresses. Every child can and should learn to make some of these decisions for himself.

Depending on your child's knowledge and experience, you as an adult can supply the necessary information, or help your child find it. For example, if it's the middle of July and you live in a hot climate, the suggestion that radishes are a cool weather crop will influence your child's decision whether or not to plant. If he decides to plant anyway, his experiences will influence him the next time—and so they should. Your older child can make more complicated choices, like deciding on rules for group competition or whether it is economically advisable to invest in new or better equipment.

A child who is allowed to make a decision will see direct results—good preparation for adulthood when consequences aren't always clear-cut, but there nonetheless.

Leaving the security of little childhood, a preteen is at once beseiged by opposite impulses. I remember it, as I'm sure you do; a desire for growth and change and at the same time the need for constancy, to know that some things remain the same.

Parents working close at hand with Nature, along with their children, can guide them to see both sameness and change. A garden is in a continual state of flux. Throughout the year there is dying and renewal, the same things happening over and over. Seeds sprout, plants grasp hold and grow strong. Flowers bud, open, turn to fruit, which provides new seeds.

In awakening, growing and dying back your garden follows another consistent natural pattern, the seasons we all delight in. Spring calls to grow, summers swell with abundance, fall brings harvest, winter its chilly hold and deathlike sleep.

In his gardening experiences with you your child will absorb the cycle intuitively. In adolescence and after, in a world of rapid change, the sameness of Nature, like long-formed habits and a solid home, can influence the way he deals with new experiences.

Along with constancy, children, like adults, need to learn an aesthetic appreciation of life—beauty for beauty's sake. And I think we all feel it's easy to miss in the middle of what is too often hectic family life.

Your garden will do much for your small child's early appreciation of beauty, and for that matter, other delights of the senses. Nature never spares color in the garden patch—from purple string beans that turn green when you cook them, to ruby colored lettuce, crimson rhubarb, scarlet radishes, blue, purple and black berries—every color and hue imagined can be there.

There is texture too—the crinkly spinach leaf, the spiny cucumber, the silky eggplant, waxy pepper, oily tomato, fuzzy peach, hard-shelled nut. From texture there is smell—heavy fragrance of the tomato plant, perfume of the fruit flowers and the aromas of each herb, from mint to oregano.

And sound too. Water bubbling down the rows, the rustle of breeze through corn stalks, hum of bees, twitter of birds and finally, toward evening, the stillness.

Nature and the garden have inspired some of the greatest thoughts expressed by man. Your child, like mine, will probably never be a Thoreau or Robert Frost, but he can learn about the beauty Nature offers to all of us.

When your child experiences success, gains independence from adults in small measure and tunes in to his personal ecology, he learns and grows as an individual. But what about social growth? Can your gardening experiences enrich your child's social growth? By all means, yes.

In the garden your child deals with Nature firsthand. But before he begins, since you are gardening together, he deals with you, in what may be an entirely new context. When much of our relationship with our children is authoritative, it can be a new and valuable experience to accept our child as an individual whose ideas and opinions are given as much consideration as our own. Gardening together provides just that opportunity. Why? Because unlike other areas of your child's life, what you do in the garden won't *change* the course of his future; successful gardening can only enrich it. That's a considerable difference.

When a child decides school isn't for him, or he's not going to do his share around the house, you're forced to use your authority as a parent. In gardening with your child, you needn't. Whether or not you plant here or there, or this or that, won't be a deciding factor in his future. So along with an attitude of encouragement rather than orders comes a relaxed feeling between us as parents and children. Your child may feel more inclined to approach with a special request, a dilemma or a confidence, while working together, than when you're perched in your chair with the evening paper. Gardening is keeping in touch without the specter of ever-present authority.

Home and Castle—The Exceptions

As soon as a child begins to participate in group play, he or she is influenced by those around. As a result, children need socially sensitive values and want to behave responsibly. What has this to do with your garden? Several things.

First, unless you live in a very rural area, there are the neighbors to consider. Having a garden is probably the least disturbing activity we can pursue in an urban area. Unless, for example, the compost heap isn't functioning as it should and odors carry for a block. Or unattended watering has flooded Grouchy Sam's backyard. Or the fallen fruit has attracted insects who don't respect the significance of fences. And so on. If there is something amiss, somebody is bound to notice and call attention to it.

So what's to be done? You can help your child learn social responsibility by planning around a minimum of inconvenience to others. "My home (and yard) is my castle" is fine in many instances, but children want to get along. Encouragement toward social responsibility will help your child learn it's easier to be friends than enemies.

Hand in hand with social responsibility comes good old-fashioned fun with friends. If you haven't tried gardening with gangs of kids, you're in for a real treat, even if you can only "indulge" once in a while. Invite your child to bring his friends. Watermelon harvest time is a natural. So's corn husking and tomato picking.

For a while, if your children are small, you'll feel like the Pied Piper. *We* have, many times. From house to garage, to garden, to compost heap, to garden, we've been trailed by five or six tiny soil-covered kids. What's so amazing, and sad too, is that you might be the only parent in thirty who is enjoying, not yelling at, the neighbor kids. And I don't think there's a child alive who doesn't feel proud when his friends are welcome in *his* yard, ooooh and aaahh at *his* watermelons and tell him, "Hey, your Mom and Dad are nice."

Finally, children need other children. Group gardening is great for kids. It gives them an opportunity to share their experiences—the frustrations and the victories—with their peers. Children will listen and learn from other children as they won't from anyone else. Group activities such as vegetable gardening let kids pit their ability against their equals, and in doing so, help each one establish himself as a person with very special talents.

Skills You'll Learn

While we're talking about learning, you are probably saying, responsibility and getting along with the neighbors is fine, but what about gardening itself?

Depending on how much time, and to a certain extent space, you and your child can devote, he or she will learn to raise many vegetables you already eat and some you'll want to try. The range of what's available to the home gardener today is enormous. Seed companies, and they are many, perfect new varieties of plants and vegetables each year. If you wish, you can grow everything from such standards as lettuce and radishes to popcorn. With proper planning, you and your child can supply much of your own food.

In growing some of your own food your child will learn what really good vegetables taste like. I don't know a child who isn't willing to try what he's had a hand in growing himself. So if your child hasn't been a vegetable eater, prepare yourself—he just may become one for the first time.

On a practical level, you and your child will learn where to get the information you need to start if you haven't gardened before; where to find land, what equipment to use, how to minimize work. You'll learn how to build the soil you want, how to decide what to grow, how to start, transplant and care for each vegetable you choose. Together, you and your child will learn to control garden pests, garden with wildlife, grow houseplants and minivegetables; and garden in containers. You'll learn about organizing group gardens, gardening for profit, and last but certainly not least, what to do with what you grow. In short, you can help your child learn about the food he or she eats, from seed to dinner table.

How to Garden with Kids and Really Enjoy It

As any interested parent knows, nothing can replace time well spent with children. The only addition I can think to make is that the time spent in the garden can be enjoyed by both.

Remember, the secret to successful gardening is simple—make the garden your child's garden from the first. Keep in mind how your child sees things, his needs as a maturing person and what he expects. Aim for success early and repeatedly.

Ready then? Let's go!

CHAPTER 2

Getting It All Together—Together

How to Garden When You Don't Know How to Start

There is probably nothing more discouraging to a would-be gardener, child or adult, than the discovery he doesn't recognize a *thing* growing in his neighbor's garden or on the vegetable start shelf at his local nursery. Not one plant resembles what we commonly serve for dinner. Not one.

Would you like to know how we learned to recognize a living tomato plant after having eaten hundreds upon hundreds of tomatoes through the years? By reading the label on the seedling—that's how! Then buying the seeds and following the growing instructions to the letter; observing the plants through all stages of growth—sprouting, first, second, third leaf stages, the transplant, flowering stage and finally fruiting—reassurance we were right.

As we expand the size of our garden each year and add new varieties, it's hard sometimes to admit our gardening beginnings were so humble—ignorant even—but they were. I couldn't tell a tomato plant from a cucumber vine.

Johnny though, and Danielle too, won't be as ignorant. No matter what vegetable makes its way into their eager mouths at dinner time, Johnny asks about it. "Are these stringbeans from the garden?" If it happens they're not, his immediate, consistent, very puzzled reply is, "Then where did you get 'em?" Yes, Mom, where else but the garden? I must tell him, "Canned from the grocery store." A puzzled expression wrinkles his brow. "But how can beans grow in a can?" he asks. Now, *that's* a good question!

Is it necessary to know something about the vegetables you want to grow? Can't we just plant, wait and see what comes up, then figure out what to do with it?

If gardening, especially vegetable gardening, were easy, I would say by all means, yes. But each plant has specialized conditions necessary for growth—full sun or partial shade, heavy or light watering, low or high soil nitrogen. Because each plant's requirements differ a little from any other plant, chances for failure can be great. Our first ignorant year we were lucky and successful, but we might easily have failed. Had we begun with Johnny in a year of failure, I can almost guarantee "Batman," as he is fond of referring to himself, would be glued to the tube more than he is, instead of prodding his paper-reading father on Saturday mornings with, "Put your boots on, Daddy, so we can go work."

To return for the moment to the original question—is it necessary to know something about the vegetables you and your child hope to grow? The answer is yes, yes, and yes again, because you *are* gardening with your children.

Fortunately, nearly everyone gardens to a degree, so it isn't hard to find someone with experience who can clue you in. If your neighbor raises vegetables, walk over for a look. Gardeners are the most sociable people I know when it comes to shop talk.

From my neighbor Sheryl, to whom we own our introduction to organic gardening, we learned about such garden delights as ruby chard, winter tomatoes, alfalfa sprouts and rhubarb, beefsteak tomatoes. We learned practical things like growing cucumbers in the corn patch, using beer as slug and snail bait, and baby food jars for hotcaps. From Sheryl I also learned to can apricots and bake zucchini bread when we were overrun the first year.

The list goes on and on. Lest you be deceived, as I had been, into thinking gardeners like Sheryl must have big gardens, let me tell you her vegetable garden measured no more than five feet by ten feet, and she lived in the city.

Besides talking to gardening friends, another sure way to learn about vegetable gardening in a hurry is to pack up the kids and visit a local nursery or grower's outlet. Nurseries are great fun for the kids. Our local nursery has *neat* things like four-foot stacks of *terra cotta* pots that sway precariously when poked. It also boasts an ornamental garden with stream and mill race that Danielle thinks is more fun than her bath on a hot afternoon.

But impending disasters aside, be sure to talk to employees about what grows well in your area, what it needs to grow and what is the easiest way for an inexperienced organic gardener to begin. In one afternoon you'll probably have more than enough information to get started, plus literature, maybe a book or two, and if your nursery man is as good a salesperson as mine, and if your children persuade like Johnny does, seeds, a sack or two of soil conditioners and a few tools. You won't doubt your time was well spent.

Reading is another way you can prepare for your first garden, and a way I know we enjoy immensely on chilly winter evenings in front of the fire.

Reading about gardening won't give you a crash course like a talk with your gardening neighbor will, but it is thorough preparation and should be ongoing. From good books on basic organic gardening you'll learn about soil structure and conditioning, water and soil management, soil pH, vegetable types and requirements, pest control and so forth. Look for children's books too. They're loaded with basic information about plant life.

A little gardening theory undoubtedly helps the gardening experience. When you know more about *why* things happen, you can begin to experiment with techniques, gradually finding those that work for you—the ones you and your children will pass on to others as your garden progresses.

The appendix of this book lists publications and books we

find useful. You can begin building your gardening library with *The Basic Book of Organic Gardening*, the one we began with. It is easy to read and explains organic techniques, such as composting, in nontechnical language. Another book chock full of very basic gardening information is *The Postage Stamp Garden Book*, about the French intensive method of organic gardening, ideal for those who wish to or must garden in a small space. A gardening encyclopedia, listing plants by common and botanical name along with their growth requirements, we've found handy when we run across something new we'd like to try and need to know how and when to get it into the ground. Watch the gardening section of your local paper, too, for gardening tips and subscribe to a regional or national organic magazine—*Organic Gardening and Farming*® is the premier publication—to benefit from the experiences of many organic gardeners.

Another source of good, compact gardening information is available to gardeners everywhere, up-to-date and free. It's the gardener's wish-book and *Bible*, the seed catalog. Seed suppliers mail catalogs usually at the start of each growing season, spring and fall. If you're not familiar with this gold mine, you'll be amazed at what you'll unearth between its covers. Many suppliers suggest which varieties afford the beginner most success because of a plant's hardiness, disease resistance or other quality that makes growing easier. Some catalogs suggest designs for different-sized gardens, helping you and your child plan around lots of vegetable variety or limited space. Some have frost and climate charts to help you choose when to plant what. They also list dates to maturity, a real asset for gardeners with either long or short seasons. The short-season gardener can count on stretching his gardening time by starting seeds indoors and intercropping. The long-season gardener can plan two or three crops and grow throughout the season. Besides seeds and plants, many seed catalogs offer an array of tools and gadgets for kitchen and yard designed to make your work easier. Even if you don't buy, catalogs are full of ideas adaptable to your garden needs and a do-it-yourselves project.

Reputable seed companies are expert in what they produce and you can feel confident following their suggestions, providing, of course, you know it's in tune with organic gardening practice. (Don't use chemical pesticides, obviously, no matter how good or safe they say they are.)

To get catalogs each season, write the company (addresses in appendix), or have your child write. P.S. Kids *love* to get mail.

Other sources of information include agricultural extension services of universities and U.S. government publications, many of which are free. Your congressman has home and garden booklets available to his constituents without charge. Just write his office. But when using government sources, be wary of nonorganic practices. We use these publications because the information about plant growth requirements and identification of diseases and pests is thoroughly researched and accurate, even illustrated. For correcting plant growing conditions, or for pest and disease control, though, consult your organic gardening material. Government publications tend to rely on chemicals, though a few are now suggesting organic practices.

Finally, if you're feeling superambitious and are the social type, you and your children can join a garden group. Many tend to specialize in certain plants, but you may be able to find one whose interest is organic vegetable growing. Watch for meeting notices in your newspaper or local gardening magazine. Members share ideas and experiences and often have speakers. Even better, perhaps, is the 4-H Club, if there is one in your area. And some Scouting projects can involve gardening, especially if you participate and lead your troop in that direction. You can also start your own organization or help your children get one going, if this side of gardening interests you. For ideas on group gardening with children, see chapter 8.

Reading about gardening and talking with those who garden will help you get a good start. When you actually get down to plans, first of all, resolve to keep your child's garden small.

Johnny's first garden was two feet by one foot. He planted it, yes. Did he weed it? No. Did he water it? Yes, when he felt like playing with the hose.

The tendency of many, ourselves included, is to think big—a dozen tomato plants instead of two, fifteen rows of corn instead of four, and so on. Your child's garden should be a size he can care for easily with your help. If your kids are small, you'll do most of the work, so resist the temptation to take a tiller to the whole backyard the first year.

When we till this spring, the kids' garden will be about three feet by four feet—a little larger than last year's two-foot by three-foot plot. There'll be room for a tomato plant, several bush beans, a few stalks of corn, radishes and some onion sets. Anything else will be grown in containers, like the mini-vegetables.

If your son or daughter decides he or she needs more space, add it a small section at a time. It's better not to start rows at all than to have them fail from neglect.

One couple we know who garden with their child have an ingenious method for deciding how large their son's garden should be. They lay him down on the ground north to south and mark off his length from head to foot. Then they lay him east to west and mark off his length again. Then they rope the area off.

Their theory, one which seems to work, is that Arlin is able to reach with his arms one-half his length. Therefore, by making the garden measure his height in each direction, he can reach anywhere from the sides of his garden patch!

The same principle can be applied when laying out gardens with older children. Use their height for each side of *several* garden areas. They'll be able to grow more vegetables in this "intensive" arrangement, since you won't need to leave room for mechanical row building.

By beginning your child's garden small, there simply won't be much garden to care for. Your small child is less likely to feel overwhelmed when facing garden chores that take only a few minutes to do. The same applies when *you* must take over where he or she left off.

If your child is older, advise a small garden nonetheless, especially if it's his or her first. For your ten-year-old, six feet by six feet or less, depending on your child, should be about right. You may well have a larger family garden that offers plenty to do if his own isn't enough. And of course there's always next year. Each year we expand a little; each year we're glad we didn't overextend.

While you're planning small, take time to think of ways to make your work easier. Some gardeners think unless they're breaking their backs they're not working hard enough to be rewarded. Nonsense!

Working with your children in the garden should be relaxing, not punishing. Watering our family garden in the 100 degree plus summer heat waves can be a problem. With twenty or more rows to water at ten minutes each, and the garden spigot 300 feet from the patch, that's a lot of time and trekking. We can't immediately do anything about the spigot. But we now construct rows so we have only to place the hose at one end (the high side) to have water flow throughout without moving the hose. We place vegetables requiring less water on the high side where they can be skipped if needed. Simple? Yes. But it did take planning from the beginning. Look for similar shortcuts in your child's garden, like a sprinkler in the center.

With your preparation behind you, you and your child are undoubtedly ready to strike out for the backyard armed with a ball of string and some stakes. All of which is fine, but what if you don't have a backyard? Or if the one you have is already landscaped?

Where to Find Land If You Don't Think You've Got Any

There are several ways to get the space you need for your child's garden. You can 1) beg it, 2) borrow it or 3) steal it. The latter we don't recommend, but you can get around that by "making" your own.

Begging for land begins with assessing what you've done with the land you've got and being willing to sacrifice an ornamental plant here and there for one you can eat (which may be ornamental as well).

Nearly every gardener has some wasted space—a bare spot or bed with some plants which could be culled to make room for your child's garden. To begin Johnny's, first we ripped up a section of lawn, replacing the crabgrass with corn. We didn't miss it at all.

When begging land from your stingy yard, however, bear in mind that a corner in full shade with inadequate drainage won't work. Success is vital. The space you choose must do more than just support plant life—it should flourish! Most of the vegetables you and your child will be growing require, at the very *least*, six hours of direct sunlight each day. If you must beg from the shady fern garden or the sunny rose garden, choose the rose garden.

For your child's mental well-being and your future relationship both in and out of the garden, choose a spot that is reasonably accessible for your child at his age. He or she shouldn't have to risk life and limb trying to reach his garden through your thorny pyracantha thicket, nor should you have to suffer as his feet tread within centimeters of your prize orchids.

If you're lucky enough to have a choice of several locations, fertile soil is always preferable to marginal soil, south or west locations will probably mean more hours of sunlight, a higher spot better drainage, and closeness to spigots and storage areas, convenience.

Watch too for those things that are so obvious they are often overlooked. We started our first family garden before the winter sun had rotated to its summer position. Cornered by a fence along the south and east sides, the sunline fell beautifully for winter gardening. But it shaded the tomato plants midsummer.

Again, planting in the very early spring, we managed to forget that the peach tree in the center of the garden would be fully leafed out in May. While we could still plant underneath it, it proved to be a better place for lettuce than the peppers and zucchini we tried there. The moral: Try not to overlook something so obvious as a large tree in the middle of the garden!

If you've searched your entire domicile and can say with reason you don't have any space for your child's garden, take a look around your immediate neighborhood and think about phase two—borrowing your land. Your next-door neighbor or someone else close by might have a weedy corner he'd be more than willing to lend, especially for an occasional sack of fresh vegetables that, your child can inform him, aren't hazardous to his health.

Privately owned vacant lots are another source of garden space. Check with your city or county to get the owner's name, then seek permission. Many people lend free vegetable garden space. You probably won't meet much resistance, but bring your child along anyway, if you ask in person. Few can resist a child's enthusiasm for a new project.

For the landowner who doesn't recognize instantly that organic gardeners like yourselves are great folk and responsible, pointing out the advantage of having part of his land cultivated for free instead of paying someone to till or mow each spring and fall to prevent fines might help. If not, try the owner of the next vacant lot.

While you're checking with local officials for owners' names, ask about public land also. Many cities have free land use for anyone wanting to start a garden.

Community gardens are springing up everywhere—often well-organized and, believe it or not, federally, state, county, city or university financed, often through revenue sharing—our April tax dollars recycled!

Just this week our local paper carried a notice from a community gardening organization *seeking* applicants interested in using their land. In many cases all you have to do is ask—the land, sometimes the equipment, seeds, soil building materials and know-how are waiting.

If you're not sure whether there are community gardens in your area, check the phone book under "ecology" or a related category. This morning I called an ecology group whose phone listing said nothing about gardening and got the names of three community garden projects and a preschool with a garden, and as yet I haven't checked the university agricultural extension, the city or the county.

When you've exhausted these resources and find you're truly ensconced in asphalt, don't give up. There is still a way.

You and your child can create your garden area and place it where you will—on a rooftop, balcony, window ledge or box, or patio. You can build permanent growing beds, or garden in containers. Cultural requirements, though different for each plant, are basically simple—enough sunlight, air, water, and soil rich in plant nutrients. Whatever your space problems, you *can* have a garden with your child.

A Parent-Child Guide to Gardening Equipment

Once you and your child have decided where the garden will be, it's time to look at gardening equipment.

The range of gardening implements is vast and, as in most selections, some are good, some less so. Just how fancy does equipment for your child's garden have to be? The answer to that is: not fancy at all—the more simply designed and sturdier, the better.

If you don't have equipment, first take a look at what you'll be doing in your child's garden, who will be doing it, and what will do the job. The latter is important. What you use to do a job and what tool your child can manage for the same job might be altogether different. Every child should have a tool for every likely task.

For example, Johnny uses a hand trowel almost exclusively. He's simply too small to handle even a little shovel. But he doesn't break up hard ground—we do. The trowel works very well for the small-scale digging he does. Our daughter uses a large kitchen spoon and pail.

Another tool small children manage very well is a hand cultivator, the tool shaped like a claw. Little children tend to work very close to the ground, unlike us older folks with weak backs. The cultivator makes a great pint-sized rake.

A third tool Johnny uses from time to time is a hand weeder. Not for weeds, but in a similar manner he can harvest radishes and lettuce without breaking the tops off. He pushes it into the ground, lifts and out pops the vegetable—intact.

A tweezer makes a handy item for kids and grownups alike. A scissors-type tweezer is useful to thin tiny carrots or onions started from seed, and other vegetables sown too closely together.

There are quite a few tools for children hitting the market now, made, as you can guess, by the toy manufacturers. At present, the only item we have is a blue and red plastic wheelbarrow. Johnny uses it primarily for riding his sister around the "back 40." Come harvest time he wheels his produce back to the house in it, which for some reason he prefers to carrying it in a sack.

We're seriously considering buying garden equipment for the kids as they reach school age. In looking we'll be keeping in mind the following:

Ariens

The right tool gets the job done more easily, but proper supervision is crucial.

Children experience the same frustrations we do when equipment breaks or isn't adequate to the job. Make sure you choose *tools*, not toys. Both are made by the same manufacturers. Check for sturdiness, first of all. Materials in kid's tools should be the same as yours—steel rather than plastic, the fewer parts the better, with stress points strongly reinforced.

Safety is one reason we insist on high quality materials to the exclusion of some touted to be "safer," plastics. Hard plastic splinters like glass and is almost as sharp. Pliable plastic simply isn't tough or sharp enough to do a gardening job adequately. Children in a frustrating situation don't stop there, unfortunately. Ours slam, bang and throw things in an effort to make them perform. Then they look for something else—like a chisel or a 20-ounce hammer—something that *will* work. The results are: cuts, bruises and bandaged fingers, to say nothing of lost tools.

Opt for a good steel implement with an edge sharp enough to work. Safety depends on good equipment and parental supervision. Heavy hammers and chisels shouldn't be left around, sure. But no parent can watch everything. If you don't give your child a poor substitute in the beginning, he probably won't have to search for a "better" poor substitute in the end.

Tool safety around the garden for us means the right tool, in the right place, at the right time, for the right purpose. Let your small children know that their tools are real, sharp and that you expect them to be used carefully. Then set a good example.

Older children should be using adult tools. If your children haven't reached a good height, you can shorten tool handles to make them more manageable, if you want to invest in another set. Some children manage adult implements simply by holding them differently. The same goes for power equipment—teach your children how to use it properly. Johnny now "helps" his father till when we can borrow the equipment. When we finally purchase a tiller and the children are old enough, they'll learn how to use it themselves, including cleaning and maintenance.

Watering for any gardener can be a large job, partly because it is so continual. For small children take a look at watering cans instead of hoses. We've been treated to more showers than we cared to when a hose has "taken off" like an angry snake in inept hands. A watering can will distribute water evenly over an area and can be handled easily. They can be heavy when filled, so buy according to your child's strength.

For watering seedbeds we use a "mister" with a trigger that delivers a fine spray. Kids love these and can use them to top water their tiny gardens.

Older kids can use hoses, sprinklers, cans sunk into the ground, Rain Birds, trenches or drip systems—whatever, depending on what's planted and what system they'd like to try. Think seriously about mulching to help retain moisture. It will greatly cut down on the amount of water needed, and your child is apt to be more conscientious about watering if it's an easy task.

Adobe to Loam—Making the Soil You Want

No matter where you put your child's garden or what equipment you invest in, it won't grow beans (literally and figuratively) if your soil isn't in good shape. It is so important that volumes have been written about soil, its structure and management for the home garden. Heavy tomes have been devoted to composting alone, which seems to say two things: First, soil, its management and composting are very important, and second, there are *many* ways to go about it.

When we decided to start our first garden, we tried to pick the most likely spot. Since there was only one area not planted in grass, we chose that. It had one advantage—plenty of sand under a sheet of black plastic that the previous owner had used as a foundation for his above-the-ground swimming pool. You've probably guessed the disadvantage. It was packed hard as rock.

There was another disadvantage we didn't discover until we took a pickaxe to the spot to break the soil up. There lay hundreds of pieces of red clay pottery broken and scattered throughout. Thinking they were left by a sloppy gardener, we forged ahead undaunted. It wasn't until several years later, when the condition of our soil had greatly improved through organic methods, that we learned the solution to the mystery of the broken pottery. Our entire subdivision was built on an old roadbed, which had a foundation of red clay pottery sunk into the subsoil!

I relate this tale just to convince you it doesn't really matter *what* you start with. Your organic methods—if you use them diligently—will improve even a problem soil like ours—even if you don't recognize it as a problem in the first place.

The first soil quality most gardeners are interested in is "tilth," or feel. Classifying your soil into one of eight types accurately isn't necessary for your child's garden. Knowing its general type, though, will tell you what you need more of to improve its tilth. Sandy soils require some moisture retaining material such as peat; clay soils, more sand for drainage.

The general soil types you and your child will be interested in are sand, clay and loam. A sandy soil will lose water rapidly, causing nutrients to leach away before plants can absorb them. Clay soil is composed of densely packed minute soil particles. Water has difficulty penetrating and once in the soil will not drain adequately, making for waterlogged conditions. Clay cracks and checks on the surface; it is brittle, not crumbly like loam. A loamy soil is ideal—a combination of different-sized particles that together help soil retain enough water, and in it, the dissolved nutrients plants need. Loam is porous enough for good air circulation, and friable—soil with adequate drainage, not too fast or too slow.

Your soil is probably a combination of these types. You can make a fairly accurate estimate by feeling it after a rain. Sandy soil will feel gritty and damp, loam will feel moist, yet crumbly, clay will feel sticky and wet. Loamy soil will have the best tilth.

Whichever you decide your soil is, giving it good tilth will make your child's garden more successful. Fortunately, the method for improving it in most cases is the same, which simplifies matters considerably. The soil best for plant growth is four to six percent organic matter (decayed vegetable matter). Even small amounts of this material will turn light colored soils to a rich brown or black. Adding organic matter in large quantities will improve the tilth of loam too, since it continues to break down over the years.

The heart of any soil-structure improvement program is the compost pile, for which organic gardeners are famous. If you don't have one, make it one of the first gardening projects you and your child begin.

Basically, compost is partially decayed organic matter such as animal manures, grass clippings, leaves or kitchen refuse. In the compost pile, microbial action converts these into "compost." The final product you turn into the garden to improve its humus content and therefore its tilth.

From exactly what, and how, an organic gardener builds his compost pile is as individual as a family recipe. Whatever method you use, the result of good techniques will be the same—lots of humus for your garden.

For a garden the size of your child's, use an amount of grass clippings or leaves that would fill a garbage can. Pile half of these on the ground and cover with an inch of garden soil, whatever the type. Next, we add bone or blood meal and top that off with an amount of manure equal to the amount of clippings. We add more soil, clippings, meal and manure in layers, then cover the whole pile with a thin layer of soil. Kitchen wastes go on top. We keep our compost pile sprinkled down in hot weather and turn it every week or so. I'm not sure how scientific our method is, but it works. In six weeks all but the largest chunks have decayed sufficiently to work into the garden. Yours should do the same.

Some gardeners have good luck with "sheet composting." Here, organic materials are added to the soil directly, turned in, then allowed to decay. Sheet composting is somewhat easier since you can do everything at once—compost, fertilize and till. Either method should work for your child's garden.

Before I leave compost piles, I must warn you. One afternoon after a rare half-hour's peace and quiet, I decided to find out what had become of Johnny. I spotted him sitting in the midst of the compost pile, busily putting things in his pockets. I couldn't imagine what, and frankly, didn't care to think about it. I'd already washed and dried countless sow bugs, beetles and bird feathers. My parental curiosity got the better of me—I wandered out. The great intrigue of the compost pile? He held up red, wriggling, fat fishing worms his fishing-partner father had shown him lived there.

We battled, then compromised. I'd let him play *if* he put the worms in a can and promised to release them in good condition later, and *if* he agreed to a bath when he was through. I doubt playing on the compost pile is likely to be recommended as ideal for children by the child specialists, but my kids think it's great, and so far we haven't met with disastrous results. To add a warning to my general warning about compost piles—they can be *hot* when in rapid decomposition, so check it out first.

Intriguing or not, no child is going to be willing to wait for the compost to finish before getting those delightful new seeds into the ground. So, what do you do?

Plan another trip to your friendly nursery. In lieu of finished compost, use peat moss, sand if you need it, and air-dried steer manure to condition your soil for its first planting. For a five feet by five feet child's garden, a large sack of each worked into the top eight to twelve inches of the soil should do the job. Without a tiller it's work, but your kids can help with the dumping part anyhow, and it's well worth the effort.

As any organic gardener knows, conditioning the soil is only part of the strategy for super vegetables your first year. The rest of the magic lies in making up deficiencies your soil may have in plant nutrients. Sixteen essential plant nutrients have been identified, most derived from rich soil, some from the air. The most notable, the ones we hear about most often, are nitrogen (N), phosphorus (P) and potassium (K), usually listed on fertilizer packages by letter with a number following that indicates the percentage in the material as analyzed. Others include trace elements such as magnesium, iron and calcium.

Just how do you know which your child's garden has and which it lacks? Well, we don't, for sure.

Finding out, though, is part of the fun and challenge of organic gardening, especially with your kids. It's a great opportunity to play Sherlock Holmes. You can find out about your soil in a number of ways.

First you can send a sample to a test lab or agricultural university where it can be analyzed for a fee. Some farm advisory bureaus across the country will run the test free of charge. In our area, though, a large agricultural center, the costs and time required to meet all the requests has meant suspension of this service, so check before sending samples.

Another way to find out what your soil lacks is to grow vegetables in it and see how they do. This, though, requires considerable knowledge of plants, their needs, and what they look like when deficient in a certain nutrient. While probably not a good way to test the soil from the beginning, observing the vegetables you grow will help you and your child spot an occasional soil problem.

A third means of finding out what your soil needs is to

test it yourself with a soil test kit that you buy. The kits vary in size, and accordingly in price, depending on how many nutrients you will be testing for. Basically you test your soil sample by adding the supplied reagent, then comparing sample color to an accompanying color chart. The intensity of color indicates the relative amount of mineral present. If you're testing for the major nutrients only and find a deficiency, begin adding an organic source, such as manure for nitrogen, then test again a month or so later. Be careful when extensive testing reveals deficiencies in trace elements. *Treating* such problems is complicated and can lead to toxicity if not done by an expert.

In general, testing soil makes an excellent gardening project for your older children (ten and up), especially if you have a budding scientist in the family. The kits are not complicated, demonstrate applied chemistry, and can be repeated at intervals with the results charted—good training in organization and deductive reasoning. Soil testing is something we'll be adding to our gardening practices as soon as the kids are old enough.

In the meantime, we deal with soil nutrients in the simplest way possible in both our garden and the children's. We just don't worry about them!

Well-rounded practices of the organic method—composting, mulching, fertilizing with organic materials and using safe methods of pest and disease control—will, in the first place, prevent many of the problems that cause the soil to become depleted. What you put into the soil will make up for, even add to, what is taken out each season by the vegetables you're going to be harvesting. All you need really is a list of which organic fertilizers supply what, and add them when you prepare the ground each season. Sound easy? It is.

For a complete list of mulching, composting and fertilizing materials, consult your basic books on organic gardening. Rather than go into those here, I'll just tell you what we use and how.

When beginning, we were on a tight budget, which was part of the reason we were starting our garden. So, first of all we looked for what was free. Lawn clippings piled in the streets for removal by the city proved a great source of mulching material and the basis of the compost pile, both. Several friends and relatives offered partially decomposed horse manure mixed with, nicely enough, oak leaves. They were overjoyed when we hauled it by the truckload. (They even supplied the truck.) Christmas that year brought very welcome gifts of oak leaf mould and peat moss, meant for the gift azaleas, but filched in part for the vegetables. As our gardening interest and knowledge grew, we bought a few small sacks of bone, blood, and hoof and horn meal, then some rock phosphate.

From there we just applied what we thought was right—a six-inch layer of manure and oak leaf, a generous sprinkling of one of the meals and rock phosphate, and we were almost ready. Each spring we clean out the ash pit from the fireplace and the wood ashes went too. That was that.

Probably the nutrient we lack, if anything, is phosphorus, since we haven't yet found a cheap source of rock phosphate what with the popularity of organic gardening on the rise. The bone meal probably makes up for any deficiency—short-term, at least.

Our plan for soil conditioning and fertilizing will probably seem haphazard to some, certainly those who use chemical fertilizers with their concomitant "numbers." But why not spend an afternoon finding out what's available to you free or at little cost, then try it for your child's garden? You'll be well on your way to a fail-proof garden.

Seed Rack, Garden Catalog and Thou—Deciding What You'll Grow

The big day is quickly approaching. The last frost has left the ground, the spring birds have reappeared, and your mouths are watering for your first squirt of ripe cherry tomatoes and buttered, juicy, sweet corn-on-the-cob.

You and your children have decided how big the garden will be, where it will go, and your soil should win a blue ribbon for fertility. Together you've worn the catalogs limp and searched the seed racks incessantly. Even you, the grownup, think you should try everything at least once. Hold it!

Before we get carried away, we sit down with the kids (well, Johnny anyway, Danielle mostly sucks her thumb), and do some regrouping. He's ready to "plant everything you guys will have in *your* garden." Here's where the most important part begins. Together we must agree what to grow, which variety, what not to and why.

Your child by this time will have a good idea of what he or she wants to grow. We make a mental list, then subject it to the "innocent-'til-proven-guilty" method.

First on his list is corn—why, we don't really know. But for the kids' garden it's a good choice. Corn germinates fast with presoaking, is large-seeded, easy to care for, hearty and note—*very important*—both kids like to eat it.

Next comes lettuce. It germinates—well—reasonably. It's not large-seeded though, but pretty easy to care for, hearty, and Johnny can't stand to eat it. You can guess our unanimous decision; he'll help us with the lettuce in *our* garden.

Radishes are next. Seeds large enough to handle, quick germinating, bright colored, hearty, quick maturing, and *I* can't stand them. The verdict? They're great for the kids' garden and I'll stick to water chestnuts in my salads.

That's how we decide what we'll be growing with our children—choosing vegetables they would like to grow, then judging each by how well we expect it to measure up to their expectations. To gain a vote for the kids' garden a vegetable must have more than a reasonable "success factor" and be interesting—either to grow or to eat, preferably both.

A basic knowledge of what grows well in your area is important too. If you've been talking with gardening neighbors, you'll probably have a good idea. Another clue is the seed racks. Anyone selling seeds in your area will be stocking something they expect will grow and be bought year after year. Seed catalogs, as mentioned before, often designate varieties that grow nearly everywhere with a symbol. They're probably safe choices.

In general, most vegetables can be grown in most areas. What makes a big difference by region is the *variety* you plant. For example, our twenty or more seed catalogs offer dozens of varieties of carrots. We've found our clay-loam soil doesn't have the "give" of a sandy soil, so we plant a "half-long" variety of carrot—one that doesn't grow (or *try* to grow) as deep. Our carrots are short, straight and plump. Not skinny and crooked as another variety might end up in our soil. Carrots are carrots, but some will do better than others in your area.

What if you and your child disagree about what to grow?

Many of your decisions about what to grow will depend on your child's age and interests. While our son tends to take our advice because he's small, your school-age children will have specific ideas of their own, some at variance with yours. That's fine. Parental insistence, after all, isn't in the spirit of organic gardening with kids. Try to grow anything your child insists on having. If you think its success factor isn't very good, just be sure your son or daughter includes other things that rate high. The vegetables following can serve as a guide. We've tried them. They're what we call "sure-fire summer vegetables."

CHAPTER 3

Sure-Fire Summer Vegetables and How to Grow Them

The chill of winter evaporates. In its stead the spring sun warms your backs in a delicious tingling. At last, preparation and planning, those imperatives to success, are behind you. Let the garden begin!

Somehow, after all the preparation, it just doesn't seem right to sow seed then wait days, even weeks for results. To your children the wait seems endless, the suspense intolerable. Yet gardens aren't born overnight. What can you do? Well, for one thing, you can let someone else do the waiting for you. You and your child can plant an instant garden.

Instant Garden for Those Who Don't Want to Wait

Invest a little your first year to take advantage of vegetable plants someone else has started, for the satisfaction of a garden overnight. We look at it this way. The gardening bug will strike for the first time in fall or winter fifty percent of the time, right? Well, if it's really bitten you and your child have planned and talked garden off and on for six months. Our son isn't yet five, which makes six months more than one tenth of his *lifetime*. Or to put things in adult perspective—three years out of thirty would be a long time to sustain anyone's interest without getting down to business! He could wait another two weeks, of course, but is it fair? We think not.

Instant gardens, instant results. They're good for everybody's morale. Whether we start with tomato plants, onion sets or eggplant, something starts the children's garden with a bang. In their affinity for the concrete, our kids turn on instantly when they *know* something is going on because, "Hey, there they are"—green plants, above ground, positive proof.

So where do you find instant gardens? At your friendly nursery, naturally. Or in the produce section of the grocery store, the plant section of the hardware store, wherever gardeners flock when the honkers head north.

Close on the heels of spring seed catalogs, the vegetable starts form ranks. These small plants should be suited to your area and are safely transplanted right away. Sure-fire summer vegetables which do well from starts are tomatoes, peppers, eggplant, strawberries, lettuce, onions, beans and chard. Choose one or several—those passing the "innocent-'til-proven-guilty" test, and your child's garden will be off to a rousing start.

Another instant garden—well, just about—can be had from presoaking larger seed. Corn or beans, for example.

Germination begins when water softens the seed coat, the first step in a series which trigger embryonic growth. (If you've ever soaked pinto beans used in Mexican cooking and forgotten them until the evening of the next day, you know about presoaking—the little green shoots make terrible frijoles but a great bean crop for next season!)

To presoak seed, cover with tepid water and let stand eight to ten hours. Presoaked corn planted in warm soil will pop up in five to six days; beans in three—almost instant companions to your child's vegetable starts.

From Small Beginnings Great Gardens Grow

Few activities in the garden are quite as exciting for children and satisfying for grownups as watching tiny seedlings pop up from soil where they've been sown with great care.

There are several good reasons for starting your own plants. First, for the large garden, starting your own seed is economical. Dollars spent for seed packets outstrip hundredfold dollars spent for several well-established plants.

A second reason for starting your own is that you're not restricted by what's available locally. Seeds are grown all over the world. In the case of rare plants, starting from seed may be the only way to get a plant your child would really like to show off.

A third reason for starting your own is the opportunity to develop second generations of plants that have done especially well the year before. That is, of course, unless you've planted hybrids. They revert to the parent strain in seeding, so stick with pure stock, if you want to improve your own strain.

The fourth and most popular reason, our favorite, is the leap on the growing season you can have by beginning plants several weeks ahead of time to set them out. In cold climates, starting indoors is imperative.

Finally, starting seeds is an activity your child can participate in from beginning to end. From building cold frames to preparing the soil, sowing seed, watering then transplanting, your child can do it all.

How to Start Your Seeds

We live in the West, in an area of moderately cold winters and hot summers. Another phenomenon is what I call "Fool's February," days of pure delight when the thermometer suddenly pops up to the 70s. Our second year in the garden we couldn't wait. Out came pails, trowels and wooden spoons, and seed packets. We enthusiastically furrowed and planted. The warm weather lasted a little over a week, just enough to give our seeds a start. Then they suffered the full clout of 20 degrees F. Needless to say, we had to begin again.

The following year we were ready. When Fool's February arrived we planted in nursery flats, milk and egg cartons. As before, the warm weather lasted just long enough to give our summer vegetables their start. We brought them in when the temperature dipped and set them out in a protected spot for the afternoon sun. By April 15, the last frost date in our area, our Fool's February garden was ready for outdoors with two months head start on the growing season.

Even if you aren't blessed with a Fool's February, you'll find your child eager to start your garden each year, especially when your seed catalogs arrive well in advance.

Egg and Milk Cartons and Nursery Flats

Start seedlings easily in planting flats. Flats, like compost heaps, can be as simple or elaborate as gardeners want to make them. We opt for the simplest, most readily available recycled materials—egg cartons, milk cartons and nursery flats.

The individual compartments of egg cartons can be planted one seed each, a job small children relish and are remarkably good at from an early age. Before planting, poke holes in the bottoms for drainage. When the seedling has reached the proper size for transplanting, (usually when it's large enough to be handled easily), your child can simply lift the seedling and rootball neatly out of its slot. He or she won't be bothered by a tangle of roots from nearby plants. Egg carton cold frames dry out quickly, so check for water every day.

Milk cartons offer a similar advantage. Good for large-seeded vegetables, plant one seed to a carton. Poke holes in the bottom so water isn't trapped. When transplanting,

A modest beginning

. . .yields an impressive produc

simply tear the sides of the carton away gently and lift the seedling with its rootball out.

Nursery flats, when you can find them, are likely to be expensive, like many items made of wood. Some nurseries are using plastic ones now; either will work. You can get them if you hunt around. We've had good luck asking for a nursery's wooden discards, broken flats for 25¢ apiece. If we find ten damaged flats, three of them can be split apart then used to repair the remaining seven. They won't make *Sunset*, but they get the job done!

Using flats, your child can start many seeds of the same kind or start several types of vegetables all at once. Put vegetables requiring similar germination temperatures in the same flat and plant vegetables that mature at the same rate together so the seedlings may be transplanted all at once. Any of the following can be started in a flat ahead of the growing season: cabbage, lettuce, onions, beans, eggplant, peppers, tomatoes, chard. Others, such as corn, carrots, cucumbers, melons and squash (including pumpkins, vegetable spaghetti and gourds), peanuts and radishes are best started in the ground since they don't transplant very well.

Mediums for Seeds

Seeds sprout best in light, moist, well-drained soil. Use a mixture of one part good garden soil, one part compost, one part sand and one part sphagnum moss. If you and your child find seedlings die off just after germination, chances are they've succumbed to "damping off," a fungus that attacks the roots or stems of emerging seedlings. Contaminated soil is the most frequent cause of infection. Sterilize your seedbed by pouring one gallon of boiling water slowly through enough soil to fill one flat. Sterilizing soil, obviously, is a parent job if your child is small. Be sure he doesn't touch the soil before it has had a chance to cool.

Another preventive measure is to start seeds in sphagnum moss or vermiculite, available at garden supply centers. These mediums do not supply nutrients, so seedlings require feeding after sprouting. Feed a liquid fertilizer made by soaking one-half cup of manure in a quart of water, or add one-quarter teaspoon of fish emulsion to a quart of water, and soak the seedbed with the liquid. When seedlings can be handled, transfer to garden area or permanent container.

You can eliminate supplemental fertilizing and prevent damping off at the same time by starting seeds in a layered cold frame. Fill a flat half full of soil mixture that has been sterilized. Fill the remaining space with a layer of sphagnum moss to within one-half inch of the top. Sow seed and water lightly. Seeds will germinate in the top layer. Just as the food supply dwindles, the roots will penetrate the nutrient-rich soil layer. You'll avoid damping off and your seedlings will have soil nutrients when they need them most. Your seeds can remain in the fertile seedbed a little longer, if you must postpone transplanting.

Helping Your Child Plant

When your soil is mixed, sterilized, cooled, damp, but not wet, your child can fill his containers and flats leaving one-half inch at the top of each for watering seedlings later on. Planting to the proper depth is easy for children familiar with measurement. Show your preschool child how to measure proper planting depth with his index finger. One-quarter inch means poking a seed down until the soil reaches the top of your child's fingernail. His first finger joint is approximately one-half inch, and the second joint about one inch.

Once sown, push soil gently over the seed and firm. Water thoroughly with a misty spray, without disturbing the seed. Cover the seedbed with clear plastic to hold in moisture and put in a protected area. Keep in mind that nursery flats filled and watered are heavy. Lift covers to ventilate (kids peeking counts too) and check for adequate moisture. When seedlings pop up, remove the covers. If evenings are still cool, replace covers at night, supporting them above seedlings with toothpicks or small sticks between the plants.

Providing Heat for Your Seedlings

Temperature may determine when seeds germinate. Most seeds simply won't start when the ground is cold. Cool weather crops generally require less heat for germination than the warm weather vegetables.

If you and your child are starting vegetables such as tomatoes, peppers and eggplant which require several weeks growing time before setting out, add a heat source to keep the soil warm, thereby speeding up the whole process. If you're handy with tools, try this:

Cut several two inch holes in the bottom of a wooden box, or use a deep nursery flat with one-half inch separations between the bottom slats. Invert the box and cut a hole in the side large enough to hold the base of a forty watt light bulb and socket in place horizontally. You can get sockets at any hardware store along with instructions for safe and proper wiring. Insert light bulb in place.

Set the seedbeds on top of the inverted box and turn the bulb on. Check the temperature of the seedbed with an inexpensive photographic thermometer.

Ideal germination temperatures vary from one seed to another, but seventy-five degrees F. is adequate for most warm weather vegetables. If the temperature is too high, try a lower wattage light bulb. If not warm enough, use a more powerful bulb. Check soil moisture every day.

Once your seeds germinate, remove them from the heating box. Ideal growing temperatures are *lower* than those for germination.

Checklist for Your Sprouting Garden

Germination rates for fresh seed are usually excellent, sometimes as high as ninety percent and above. If you and your child find your seeds aren't measuring up, or your seedlings aren't surviving after germination, ask yourselves:

Is the planting soil too heavy? Is the weather too cold? Are we letting the seedbed dry out? Is the seed packed for the current season? Have we remembered to lift the covers to let the air in? Are insects attacking the plants? Are they getting too much sun? Have we planted too deeply?

Sometimes the problem may simply be not waiting long enough. If you've checked all of the above, then chances are your seeds will flourish.

How to Transplant Seedlings

Once your cold frames and hotbeds have produced starts large enough to handle, if the weather is right you can move them to your permanent garden area.

Transplanting is reputed to be somewhat difficult, probably because inexperienced gardeners transplant under the worst conditions—like in the heat of the afternoon sun. In fact, we're surprised almost every year, because we end up with more vegetables than we planned for.

When our tomato starts were ready last season we decided on ten plants as ideal for eating and canning. We transplanted a dozen, expecting to lose at least two. They *all* grew.

Our next overly successful transplant came about after radical surgery on our very crowded muskmelon patch. The culled plants lay in a forlorn heap in the hot sun for several hours until my husband, who hates to see healthy plants uprooted, even when thinning, decided what-the-heck, and planted them in another row. Melons, even transplanted with care, have a hard time—in theory, anyway.

Well, out of the twelve or so plants we added to our garden, only two didn't make it. I continually rearranged the contents of the fridge to accommodate the extra produce. So much for the difficulties of transplanting.

The day before they are to be moved, have your child

water his starts. Transplant in the evening or after the garden patch is in the shade. It will greatly reduce plant shock.

Dig a new hole for your seedling in a well-prepared garden area. Carefully lift the start from its container, supporting it from underneath, leaving as much soil around the roots as possible.

Children are inclined to lift plants right up by the stems, so demonstrate first, if your child doesn't know how.

Gently lower the plant into the hole and fill in soil around the sides of the plant. When you've finished, water the plant gently, then add a little more soil if it settles. Wait two weeks before fertilizing.

Your plants may wilt a bit, but most adjust to new surroundings in a day or two. If you expect hot weather, shade them with cardboard until they've recovered.

The Sure-Fire Summer Garden

Just what is it that makes a child's garden sure-fire?

Besides being composed of vegetables your child likes and ones that have a high success rate, your child's garden should fulfill his or her basic expectations. Some part of your child's garden should grow fast enough to satisfy the most limited attention span; should be easy to care for; should produce abundantly; should be full of a variety of colors, textures, tastes; and should be fun—and fascinating. Too much to expect from one, albeit *small* garden? Of course not!

Certain vegetables are naturally fast starters like beans, radishes and onions.

Hurry-Up Sure-Fire Summer Garden

Beans

From the time Jack climbed his first bean stalk to the world of the Giant, the bean has been a part of children's lives as well as a part of their diet. A staple of the New World along with corn and squash, it climbed its way across the continent, firmly staking its place in American cookery. The bean belongs in your child's garden as surely as it does in history and folktales.

Beans grow as bushes or climbing vines and are called, respectively, "bush" or "snap" beans and "pole" beans. Beans of all types sprout in four to seven days in soil above sixty degrees F. They mature in six to eight weeks.

Plant in well-prepared soil, not too high in nitrogen, but with an ample supply of phosphorus and potassium. Plant bush beans one bean to a hole, one inch deep, two inches to four inches apart, with eighteen inches to twenty-four inches between rows, if you're planting in rows. Pole beans climb five feet to eight feet and need support. Plant several at the base of a rough surfaced pole at intervals of three to four feet, or grow trellised or along a fence. A favorite with children is the "teepee" hideout—several poles positioned in a circle, then lashed at the top forming a vine-covered wigwam for the neighborhood "Indians."

Water beans regularly. When using a sprinkler, allow enough time for leaves to dry before dark to avoid plant disease. Shallow cultivation or mulching completes bean care. You won't have to fertilize, but you should inoculate the seed. If you do, nitrogen fixing bacteria living on the legume roots convert nitrogen from the air to a form suitable for plants and enrich your soil at the same time—another bonus of all legumes in the garden. The inoculant—generally a black powdery substance—should be available wherever seed is sold. Dampen the seeds and sprinkle them with the inoculant just before you plant.

Beans bear throughout the season in first, second and third crops if your child picks regularly to stimulate flower production. He or she can tell if a bean is ready for harvest by feeling the pod. It should be soft at the tip, plump, but without distinct seed outline.

Invite help in the kitchen with snapping and cooking beans. Shell limas first; all others can be cooked pod and all. If you've grown the special purple bush beans or speckled limas, your child will discover that, as if by magic, the purple beans will turn green after two minutes of cooking; the limas will turn pink and, like the mythical leopard, lose their spots.

Radishes

For any child's hurry-up garden, the radish is a good choice. Radish seeds are small, roundish and compact, making them easy to sow one by one. Radishes for some (like me) may be a never-acquired taste, but they're great garden performers, and many kids eat them from an early age.

Although radishes are classified a cool weather crop, we include them in our "summer" garden because they can be planted as soon as the ground can be worked. Planted early, radishes mature before the summer heat causes them to bolt, and can be replanted after the height of summer for a fall harvest.

Radishes rate high in a sure-fire kid's garden—appearing above ground in three to four days after sowing. They mature scarlet, scarlet and white, or white, resembling icycles.

Some varieties are tolerant of heat and can be harvested into summer. Plant in friable soil, worked one inch deep with mature compost. Sow seed one-half inch deep in drills, covering with sifted compost. Water well and firm soil after planting. Pithy, small, very hot radishes are the result of too little water, so be sure your child waters liberally and often. His radishes will be firm, large and crisp.

Harvest radishes when globes are fully round and well formed. Remove green tops before storage to prevent the radish root from wilting.

Onions

If you've ever tried to grow onions from seed, you're probably wondering why we encourage our kids to make onions a part of their hurry-up garden. We weren't too impressed with onions from seed the first time we tried them, either. Then we discovered the onion "set," a tiny oval onion which is ready to eat green in salads twenty-five days after planting. Now we buy sets in hundred-count bags or by the pound and harvest them year-round in the family garden.

The kids plant their share too. Onion sets, or onion plants, have a distinct psychological advantage for kids. They look like the finished product. The set *is* a tiny onion; the onion plant *is* an onion plant. When each is left in the ground a season it matures into the large globes we're so fond of dressing hamburgers with. Easy to relate to!

Onion sets and plants can be ordered from catalogs. Their popularity with the home gardener has increased so much the last few years that instead of looking in an obscure corner of an obscure hardware store as we used to, we now buy them at the garden department of a large drugstore chain. Such is progress!

Wherever you get yours, your children will have fun planting and harvesting them. Plant onion sets one inch deep, two inches apart. Plant onion plants covering the white "bulb" and a quarter inch of stem. Prepare soil for planting with a layer of manure compost worked into garden soil. Onions need moisture, so water frequently, flooding onions in warm weather.

Your child's onions may be picked green, or allowed to grow until the tops fall over. Uproot, sun-dry for several days, then cut stems off one inch above the onion root. Bag in mesh and store, if you wish, in a dry, well-ventilated place.

Easy-Care Sure-Fire Summer Garden

Nature had children in mind, perhaps, for summer's most prolific vegetables are those kids enjoy eating most. Add that these vegetables are easily cared for and it's a sure-fire combination for your child's summer garden.

What are these garden greats? Corn, cucumbers and

pumpkins top the list, then come squash and kids' all-time favorites, strawberries.

Corn

I haven't met the child who wouldn't eat corn in some form—on the cob, whole kerneled, creamed, in fritters, or popped. Nor one with a garden who didn't have some—tall, green and tasseling—a favorite hideout for kids half its height.

Plant corn one-half inch to one inch deep in soil worked with humus or well-rotted manure, after ground is warm and evenings are frost free. Corn requires space, thirty-six inches between rows, so we usually plant on the north edge of the children's small garden where stalks can spread without shading the rest of the garden. If your space for corn is limited, you probably won't be planting too much in your child's garden. You may prefer to have separate corn space, away from the main garden area. Corn may be planted in five gallon tubs, also. If space for corn severely limits how much you can grow in your child's garden, be sure to choose an early variety so his or hers is the first to the table. For corn to pop, see chapter 7.

Press soil firmly over seed and water thoroughly. Side dress hungry stalks with well-rotted manure, mulch with straw to help retain moisture in hot weather, and water frequently.

Your child's corn is best harvested in the "milk stage." Corn ears will be filled to the tips, the silks brown. Pull back part of the husk. Prick with a fingernail. Milky juice from the kernel means corn-on-the-cob for dinner—tonight.

Cucumbers

The cucumber, along with the tomato, is one of our kids' favorites—rapid growing, flowering, heavy producing and long seasoned. Cucumbers are fun to hunt for, easy to pick, large, and can be eaten right from the garden sometimes, skin and all.

Corn

Seed.

Corn is that great All-American crop: the native American, THE big farm crop, the special treat at the midsummer picnic. Sweet corn, the best kind for eating, just has to be cooked and eaten within minutes of harvest, which makes it a natural for any garden with enough room for a few rows.

The seed should look familiar, since it is the corn kernel removed from the cob. It is seeded directly in the garden rows, and within a week the first green shoots will press their way through the soil surface. Corn grows rapidly, and despite what folks say about hearing it grow, the plant is generally pretty quiet. The plants may resemble gargantuan grasses in their early stages of growth, and in fact corn is in the same botanical family as the grasses.

The next important stage to watch for is tasseling. This is when the spindly flower appears atop the plant, and is the period of efflorescence. The tassels produce the pollen, which is carried by the wind; thus you need more than one or two rows of corn to ensure adequate pollination.

Finally one day it's got ears. They are small, but there's no mistaking them. It's got ears. This is when the waiting is difficult. But you watch the silk, and when it turns brown, the ears are ripe. Have the water boiling when that moment arrives.

Early growth.

Tassels.

The ear at midseason.

Almost ripe.

The varieties available makes them a natural for children's gardens. If you have lots of room, choose a vine and let it run. Cramped for space? Plant a climbing variety. Unlike many summer vegetables, cucumbers are sun-savers. They prefer moist, semishady areas.

Cucumbers require lots of water and plant nutrients. For your child's garden a "hill" arrangement should save space and work. Dig a hole two feet wide and two feet deep. Fill with two shovelsful of manure compost, then remaining topsoil. Plant seed four to a hill, one-half inch deep. Water thoroughly. Mulching with compost will add nutrients and help retain water. Water consistently to avoid bitterness. Pick when cucumbers are good-sized, before seeds enlarge.

Pumpkins

If there's a vegetable in the garden saying excitement's to come, it's the pumpkin, harbinger of the holidays. For grownups the ripening pumpkin means the end of a successful gardening season, time to return from barbecue to fireside, a winding down and snuggling in.

For our kids it's Halloween—ghosts, goblins, friends over for a communal trick-or-treat, topped off with pumpkin pie. Pumpkins mean pounds and pounds of exuberant garden success in the fish story tradition! So whose going to grow *this* year's biggest? Orangest? Best shaped?

Pumpkins are a member of the squash family, a warm season vegetable. Most grow on vines and require room to run. Since our space is not severely limited, we grow them away from the main garden areas, running them beneath the fruit trees. If space is a problem, plant pumpkins on the edge of your child's garden and let them spill over lawn, or even concrete—just insulate them with a layer of straw.

Plant pumpkin seeds one inch deep in soil worked with well-rotted manure. Plant in "hills," groups of four or five seeds, then thin to two plants per hill leaving the strongest vines to produce. Pumpkins, like many squash plants, require heavy feeding and ample amounts of water consistently. For giant pumpkins, your child can single out several which look promising and pick off new flowers as they bud. With fewer pumpkins competing for water and food, those remaining on the vine will be large.

Squash

Summer and winter squash are two vegetables we heartily recommend for a child's garden. (The winter varieties are grown during warm weather, then stored through fall and winter; summer varieties are eaten immature.) The bushes of the zucchini and crookneck squash are large and produce heavily.

Here's your chance to explain basic reproduction, if your child is interested. The squash plant is one of few in the garden which produce flowers of a distinct sex. The male flowers open first at the end of a long stem. The female flowers soon follow on the tip of a thick, short stalk looking like what it actually is—a small squash. After fertilization takes place, the "stem" of the female swells, elongates and produces a squash. The seeds in the new squash, of course, would produce new squash plants. To prove it, save some for next year.

Older children may be interested to learn that the flowers of the zucchini are edible. Dipped and sautéed gently, they're an unusual garden eating bonus.

To start squash seed, prepare a garden area in sandy, well-drained soil worked with mature compost. Squash plants need room, so if your garden area is small, choose the more compact, bush varieties for your child's garden. Sow summer squash seeds first, covering one-half inch deep, three feet to six feet apart. In your child's garden, a corner is usually a good spot. One month after planting summer squash, sow winter squash seeds.

Firm soil around each seed, watering liberally throughout the season. All squash plants need full sun, food and gallons of water. Top dress with manure or fertilize with fish emulsion several times during fruiting. Avoid letting summer squash get too large since table quality is best when fruit is six inches to eight inches long. Frequent harvesting encourages flower production.

Winter squash should be cared for like summer squash, but allowed to mature on the vine forming the hard shell necessary for winter keeping. Harvest just before the first fall frosts. Wash carefully, wipe lightly with cooking oil, and your child's squash will keep inside for several months.

Strawberries

The strawberry, as I've mentioned, played a large part in our early gardening experiences. This year we've begun a new strawberry bed. Johnny, in his unfailing enthusiasm for strawberries, brought me the makings of the new bed himself—our new gardening neighbors had extras. He toted them over in a plastic sack, and planted them the following weekend.

Strawberries can be started from seed, but we use plants for a fast, sure start. In general, strawberries are of two types—June bearing and everbearing. The former are ideal for canning, jam and jelly making, eating too. The everbearing, as their name suggests, bear several crops through spring and summer.

Either type will more than pay its way in your child's garden measured against the amount of care required. For best results, choose disease- and virus-resistant varieties. For smaller children the everbearers offer treats almost every day—one or two, sometimes a dishful of naturally sweet rewards for as simple garden care as watering. June bearing varieties in your older child's garden can introduce your son or daughter to stocking up early. June jam making at our house is a family project from beginning to end.

You can buy strawberry crowns at your nursery or order stock from seed companies. Buying locally may be your best

Zucchini seeds.

Zucchini

The blossom opens.

Zucchini is a green-skinned summer squash. Although this variety of squash is known by an Italian-sounding name, the squashes in general are strictly American and were among the staple crops of those Indians of the West who maintained gardens. Of all the squashes —winter, summer, acorn, Hubbard, patty-pan, and others—the zucchini is one of the most versatile and popular.

Zucchini seed is rather flat, with a distinct rim. It looks and feels very much as though it had been stamped from cardboard.

But the plant it spawns belies that idea. The plant develops as a knotty cluster of blossoms and leaf stalks. The leaves are plate sized and deep green, the blossoms yellow trumpets. When planted in fertile soil squash can get very large, spreading over a lot of ground and producing baskets of delicious fruit.

The fruits, of course, develop at the blossom, provided the flower is pollinated. As it burgeons, the zucchini looks a lot like a cucumber, but it doesn't taste like a cuke. When it is ripe, the fruit will easily separate from the stalk.

The principal squash pest is the squash bug, which feeds on the plant sap, using its needle-like mouth parts.

Early in the fruiting stage.

The squash bug.

The ripened fruit.

bet. Our favorite variety, "Shasta," isn't available in our current catalogs, but abundant at a local outlet and ideally suited for our climate.

Plant strawberry crowns in the early spring, when the ground can be worked. They do best in light, well-drained soil worked six inches to eight inches with mature compost. Set plants in soil, covering roots completely. Keep the entire crown above ground. Place plants one and one-half feet apart to allow room for runners which will root to form new plants. Fertilize with fish emulsion six to eight weeks after planting. Ideally, you should pick off flowers forming the first year to increase plant vigor and production in the following years. I'll add though, that our first year we didn't know this; the plants fruited and did just fine.

Strawberries will hog the garden if you let them. There are two solutions if they become a problem. Your child can cut off new runners, then replace three-year-old plants with the young crowns, thus keeping the number of strawberry plants constant. Better yet, plant new strawberries in containers—they're ideally suited. "Strawberry jars" are one answer; so are large redwood tubs, or long, narrow patio planters. Seed catalogs are full of other space-saving ideas for strawberries.

After your plants have started, watch closely for pests—slugs, snails and ants in particular, birds, too. (To deal with these strawberry lovers, see chapter 4.) Make sure your child keeps his berries thoroughly watered, especially while bearing. To help retain moisture and keep berries clean, mulch with straw or grass clippings. For kitchen ideas (not that you'll probably need any), see chapter 9.

Bright and Hearty Sure-Fire Summer Vegetables

For all of us, color delights the senses, whether the subtle hues of hayfields against a pinking blue sky at sunset, or close-at-hand garden colors, which would serve no finer purpose than the pleasure they give—the orange-and-fern-green of the carrot, the purply-gloss of the eggplant, the red-veined-green of ruby chard, or scarlet-on-green of the tomato.

Nor is color the sole offering of these garden sure-fire vegetables. They bear up, and *generously*, in less than ideal conditions. They can withstand some of the neglect that is part and parcel of most gardens.

Carrots

Without a doubt, this one's special. Johnny uproots a few each evening, twists off the tops, washes them with care at the bathroom sink, then doles them out to his sister in a rare moment of generosity. Flavor-wise they can't be beat—natural sugar unparalleled in any produce department I know. All others should be labeled imitation.

Carrots are easy to grow in almost any type of soil if the bed is prepared. Work before planting with mature compost. Don't use raw manure or the tiny roots will burn. Sandy, uniform loam is best, but we've grown half-long carrots successfully in clayey soil.

Carrot seed is very tiny so you may have to help your child plant. (From experience I'd advise against sowing on windy days!) Sprinkle seed from the packet into a small indentation running the length of your furrow. Cover with fine soil one-fourth inch deep. Sprinkle down with a soft, very gentle spray, and avoid letting seed dry out during germination. (Here in California, that means watering morning and evening.) When carrots begin to look crowded, thin to three inches to four inches apart. In a well-prepared bed, your child's carrots shouldn't need fertilizing. Flood the carrot bed frequently through the summer.

Your child can leave his carrots in the ground until the first fall frost. If he or she hasn't eaten them all beforehand, carrots can be pulled, the tops removed, roots stored cool and moist for winter use.

Eggplant

This vegetable is probably one of the most beautiful grown. Its leaves have the soft, supple feel of quality leather. The eggplant grows in soft greens and purples, flowers yellow and bears black, shining fruit. It's one of the kids' favorites to watch and harvest. A versatile casserole staple, we serve it often—sautéed with tomatoes, green peppers and mushrooms.

If you wish to start eggplant from seed, begin indoors eight weeks before time to set out after the last frost. Eggplant should be placed in a well-drained, fertile area in full sun. Transplant to a hole partially filled with fine, mature compost. Spread eggplant roots, water, fill with additional compost and firm soil. Water again. Plants should be spaced forty-eight inches apart. Shading newly planted seedlings will prevent wilting. Harvest fruit when the skins are highly glossy. Use soon after picking.

Swiss Chard

For heartiness and color Swiss chard is one of the best vegetables your child can choose. Standard green varieties are patterned with cream-colored veins; ruby chard is brilliant—wine-colored leaves, crimson veined, atop scarlet stalks. Chard tastes similar to spinach and is high in vitamin A. It can be wintered over by covering with a heavy straw mulch, and if not mulched, will withstand a light frost. Teach your child to pick only the outer leaves. The immature center leaves will mature quickly, providing a full season's eating from just a few plants.

Swiss chard is actually a small rooted beet with large edible tops. Its hard seed should be presoaked in compost water for twenty-four hours before planting. Chard does best in a well-drained garden area in full sun. Dig several inches of compost into the row, and if soil is very acidic, add some lime.

Plant seed one inch deep in rows twelve inches apart. Thin to eight inches to twelve inches between plants. For serving ideas your children will like, see chapter 9.

Tomatoes

A member of the nightshade family, the tomato was shunned for centuries. Acute hunger probably forced the first human to taste this tempting fruit and risk the consequences. Within 400 years, the tomato progressed from reviled to relished. For good reason, it's the most popular "vegetable" grown in the home garden.

Starting tomatoes indoors or in cold frames outside is one of our first gardening projects with the kids. Sow seed one-half inch deep or less and cover with sifted compost-soil mixture. Water with a gentle spray and cover. When seedlings have emerged, remove their covers, but keep the plants in a protected area. When the small tomato plants can be handled easily, move to a well-drained garden area in full sun, preferably where tomatoes have not been grown before. Transplant on a cool day, or after sunset to prevent shock.

Dig a hole large enough for the roots to spread, and fill the bottom with fine humus compost. Set tomato plant root ball into the hole, filling it with the remaining soil and compost. Soil should reach one inch higher up the stem than it did originally. Water thoroughly, firm soil down. If the weather is hot, shade plants to avoid shock.

Soon your child's tomato plants will put forth a profusion of tiny yellow flowers. The small tomatoes will appear close after, near the stem, in place of the withered flowers.

Avoid setting plants out too early, since nighttime temperatures must remain above 60 degrees F. for plants to set fruit. Your child should water tomatoes infrequently. Lush vine with no fruit can be the result of overwatering. If your child's plants aren't producing, let the soil dry before giving

Seeds.

Fruit development beginning

Seedlings.

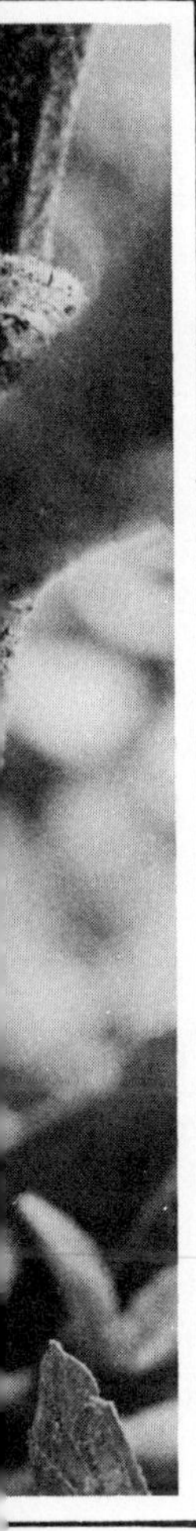

Nearly ready.

Eggplant

Eggplant should be started indoors. Some doggy day in February, March, or April, depending upon where you live, sow the oddly shaped eggplant seeds into flats and get them started a-growing. Within 8 to 10 weeks, if you've figured correctly, both the plants and the weather should be ready for the move to the garden.

The plant is related to both tomatoes and peppers, and the thriving plant does resemble the pepper plant, though the texture and shape of the leaves are markedly different. The most prominent eggplant pest is the flea beetle, which may descend upon your plants in clouds and thoroughly perforate the leaves. These minute insects can *stunt the plants, but clearly some holes in the leaves don't hurt. Don't overreact with the rotenone.*

The curiously pretty little blossoms quickly give way to relatively enormous egg-shaped fruits. While the fruits are usually purple, yellow and white varieties are available and were, during the Middle Ages, very widely cultivated. The fruits should be picked before they lose their gloss.

Everything about eggplants—from the appearance of the fruit to the look of the seed—is interesting, odd, or funny, some might say. The versatility and taste of eggplant is no exception. It is used commonly in European cooking, but less so in America. It's an excellent dish for some doggy day in fall, when you want something interesting.

more water. (Even in blistering 108–110 degree heat, we rarely water more often than every four to seven days.)

An excess of nitrogen in the soil can be another cause of abundant vine, but little fruit. Unless your soil is severely nitrogen deficient, you won't need to feed tomatoes. In normal soil, tomatoes do well with a layer of compost mulch around each plant. Additional feeding isn't necessary.

Your child can pick tomatoes as they ripen. Before the fall frosts, pick off unblemished green tomatoes and wrap them in newspaper. Store them in a cool place. They'll ripen off the vine one by one into November.

Fun and Fantasy Sure-Fire Summer Garden

Most of the vegetables in your child's garden thus far are ones which you would be likely to grow in your family garden. What makes a garden especially fun for a child are those vegetables which also make it different—additions we call fun and fantasy vegetables: edible soybeans, peanuts, rainbow corn, sunflowers, vegetable spaghetti, watermelon, the long and serpent cucumbers, and yard long beans. They're most fun after your child is familiar with more common vegetables.

Edible Soybeans

The soybean has been a valuable part of the Asian diet since 2800 B.C., but a relative newcomer to the western hemisphere, making its first appearance in 1854. Vegetable soybeans can be used green like lima beans, or dried and roasted like peanuts for a nutritious snack. They require a long, warm growing season to reach full maturity. If your growing season is short, your child can still enjoy soybeans. Plant an early maturing variety, and pick them in the green stage.

The culture of soybeans is similar to that of other snap beans. Soil should be rich, though not heavy in nitrogen. You can add some lime if your soil is very acid, and work beds with bone meal and wood ashes before planting.

Tomato

Seeds.

Everyone loves an underdog, and maybe that's why America loves the tomato. For the tomato was once the object of general suspicion. As recently in history as 1900, George Washington Carver could shock people by calmly devouring whole tomatoes. Ostensibly the scientist did it to prove tomatoes were not poisonous, as many believed, but it's just as likely that he ate them because they were — and still are — really tasty.

Carver must have made the point, for today all across America, boys and girls and men and women grow tomatoes. Lots of them don't grow anything else, just tomatoes. And they grow tomatoes themselves because the grocery-store variety simply doesn't compare to the vine-ripened kind.

Ambitious gardeners begin with the seeds, starting them in flats indoors. Others purchase seedlings—sometimes called starts. In either case, when the baby tomato plants are solidly established and when the weather is just right the seedlings can be transplanted into the fertile gardening soil.

There the seedlings will burgeon and grow. In fact, the plants sometimes get out of hand, sprawling over the ground, sprouting roots wherever stems touch the earth, concealing their fruits. Some gardeners tie the plants to supporting stakes or trellises, and others carefully break off whatever they deem to be extraneous foliage.

The real fun—the eating—begins when the fruits fill out, big and red and juicy.

Seedlings.

Tomato hornworm fatally parasitized.

Blossoms.

Big, red, juicy
vine-ripened tomatoes.

Plant soybeans one inch deep with twenty-four inches between rows. Thin plants to four inches apart after sprouting. For green soybeans, your child should harvest when the beanpods are two-thirds grown and before they turn yellow. Parboil beans in the pod for five minutes, to make shelling easier.

Edible soybeans left to mature should be dried on the vine, then picked immediately, while the stems are still green. Shell dried beans, spread on a tray and heat in the oven at 135 degrees F. for 30 minutes to one hour. Allow to cool and store in tightly sealed jars. For soybean snacks, see chapter 9.

Peanuts

The peanut, a favorite kid snack, is nutritious and fun to watch grow. The peanut plant is a vine that produces two sets of flowers. The first set, yellow, and resembling those of the pea plant, are pretty but sterile. Shortly after, fertile, hardly noticeable flowers appear. From these flowers, long shootlike protrusions called peduncles reach out and downward, burying themselves in the soil. At the tip of each, underground, a new peanut will grow.

Peanuts require a warm, sandy location and a long season. Peanuts can be grown in the north, but do best there with a southern exposure. Shell the nuts and plant three inches apart, one and one-half inch deep. Water and keep peanut bed weed-free. The soil should be loose, so peduncles can go underground easily. In warm climates, dig peanuts when foliage begins to yellow. The inside of the peanut shells should be veined and show color. Hang vines, or spread peanuts on wire screening for two months to cure. In the north, leave peanut vines standing until mid-October, then dig up. Hang vines in a well-ventilated attic. For roasting and other peanut ideas, see chapter 9.

Rainbow Corn

If your children are interested in making things from materials their garden can supply, they will really enjoy rainbow corn. In combination with pumpkins, gourds and sunflowers, the decorations they can make are limited only by their lively imaginations. These corn varieties are grown as ornamentals only, and are not much good for eating. Plant them *away* from edible corn varieties to avoid cross-pollination.

Prepare, plant and cultivate ornamental corn as you would edible corn. Harvest ornamentals later than edible varieties, when kernels are past the milk stage. Pull back and tie husks. Hang them to dry for several weeks. Your child can paint them with clear lacquer to brighten the kernels and hold them firmly on the cob.

Sunflowers

For a fantasy garden, the sunflower takes the prize. It's eerie. Somehow walking beneath a flower that towers some twelve feet above ground—seven feet above my head, ten feet above my son's, invites games of imagination such as "What do you suppose would happen if . . ." Giant flowers, giant insects, apples the size of basketballs, tree tops invisible through the clouds. What would happen if our relative size were to drastically change? Children's answers are fascinating; after all, theirs by comparison *is* a small world! Ask them.

Besides speculation, sunflowers in the garden mean good snacking. The head of the sunflower, measuring nine inches to fifteen inches in diameter, is filled with row upon row of sunflower seeds, rich in B vitamins and the food energy kids need.

Plant sunflower seeds (viable seed, not the roasted variety), two weeks before the last frost in soil rich in humus, on the north side of the garden, where they won't shade other plants. Sow seed directly into the garden one-half inch deep

Seed.

Blossoms.

The farmer is interested in the cash soybeans bring in; livestc feeders, in the protein the bec provide; and industrialists, in oil the beans yield. But you, gardener, are interested in flashy plant that yields ta meals, and that's the soybean.

Soybeans are easy to grc hard to harvest. But they tremendously valuable plants, they add to the fertility of soil in which they grow, and seeds are very nutritious—a tasty—eating.

As legumes, soybeans have ability, when properly inoculat to fix nitrogen from the air store it in nodes on the pl roots. Left in the ground harvest time, the roots decomp and the nodes add their nitro to the soil. Proper inoculat merely means sprinkling a of a special powder, available most seed stores, on each s before planting. If planted good soil and inoculated, s beans won't need extra ferti ing.

Soybeans develop rather slc ly, growing hairy oval leaves a heavy clusters of pods with t or three beans in each pod. T pods can be harvested green, best approach for those liv

Soybeans

Green pods.

where the growing season is short. Or the plants can be permitted to die and dry before the pods are picked. The pods yield the beans grudgingly, but more so when they are green.

The nutrition your soybeans provide and the way they taste in your favorite bean dishes, however, make up for the trouble you'll have. Besides, they were easy to grow!

in rows three feet apart. When plants are up, thin to two feet apart in the rows.

Let sunflowers remain in the garden until thoroughly ripe. The back of the sunflower head will be brown and dry. Birds find ripening sunflowers better than average forage, so you might want to cover the heads of your child's crop with cheese cloth to discourage marauders. You can also cut off the ripening heads while the backs are still slightly green and allow them to dry thoroughly where the birds can't get at them. They can be hung in an attic from a foot or two of stem, if space is a problem. Remove the sunflower seeds from the flower with a stiff brush, fish scaler, or little fingers (our favorite method). For eating ideas see chapter 9.

Vegetable Spaghetti

Long twisty forkfuls of spaghetti with your family's best homemade sauce is probably one of your children's most-asked-for meals. It is at our home. Johnny, in his usual mealtime manner, would ask, "Where does spaghetti grow?" For a long time, I would answer that gardens don't grow spaghetti. All that's changed now that we've discovered and grow vegetable spaghetti.

This vegetable is a member of the squash family—a real newcomer to the produce section if available at all, and still listed in catalogs under "unusual vegetables." Kids like it, it's versatile, and much lower in calories than spaghetti, with a very similar flavor. We fully expect it to become a staple with many gardeners; it is with us.

Vegetable spaghetti grows best in conditions suitable for other squash plants. Plant after frost in warm soil worked with compost, one inch deep in hills, in a sunny location. Like other squash plants, vegetable spaghetti is prolific with plenty of sun, water and nutrients. Harvest when rind is hard and fruits are oblong and golden. Spaghetti squash can be stored inside at 55 degrees F.– 65 degrees F. Leave part of the stem attached for better keeping. For eating ideas your kids will like, see chapter 9.

Watermelon

Summer wouldn't be summer on the farm without watermelon eating contests. *All* kids deserve a watermelon summer! For growing satisfaction and eating fun, this melon is worth every inch of space it requires. If you're really confined, you can grow midget varieties (see chapter 7). So don't leave this one out.

Watermelons like loose, well-drained, warm soil. They require copious amounts of water, for obvious reasons.

Start seeds indoors at 85 degrees F. three to four weeks before time to set out. Plant seed one-half inch deep and cover with fine soil. Transplant to garden area when weather is warm and fertilize with manure compost. If you wish to start them outdoors directly, plant two inches to three inches apart, several seeds to a hill. Thin, keeping the most vigorous plants to produce.

Extra Long and Serpent Cucumbers

The extra long cucumber grows fifteen inches to twenty inches in length and is slender, with warty looking skin. If your child likes giant vegetables, try this one. It can be grown on a fence or trellis to save space.

The serpent cucumber grows up to four feet in length, coiling 'round and 'round itself like a basketful of snakes. My son would describe it as "squirmally," after a toy with similar characteristics!

Plant the seeds of both varieties after frost, in warm ground well worked with manure compost. Space six seeds in a hill, hills six feet apart. Thin to three vigorous plants per hill. Cultivate shallowly and water liberally. Pick off ripe fruit to encourage production throughout the season.

Yard Long Beans

Another fantasy vegetable in the giant category is the asparagus, or yard long bean, which sports edible pod clusters up to two feet long. A pole bean variety, the yard-long bean is well suited to a wigwam arrangement. Set poles before planting beans.

Plant in smooth soil not overly rich in nitrogen where other beans will grow. Plant seeds one inch to one and one-half inches deep, one and one-half inches apart in rows two feet apart. Press soil down firmly. Harvest pods while tender and cook immediately. Yard long beans can be planted in July for an additional fall harvest.

Sure-Fire Summer Garden—
Everybody's Favorites You'll Want to Try

Lettuce and peppers are so much a part of the summer garden, it's hard to imagine a garden without them. While several vegetables are more exciting than lettuce for your child to grow, somehow a few heads seem to round out an otherwise complete garden.

Taste-wise, I'm not sure peppers appeal to most children from an early age (at least not in this country), but they're hearty, prolific and colorful. If either of these garden standbys meet the "innocent-'til-proven-guilty" test, by all means include them in your summer garden.

Lettuce

Lettuce is a cool weather crop. To include it in our summer garden, we plant it early and in partial shade, then harvest before the full clout of summer heat. Some varieties are more heat-tolerant than others. Choosing a variety which is slow to bolt will prolong your lettuce crop in warm areas.

Lettuce does well in almost any well-drained soil. Work bed shallowly with compost before planting. Sow seed thinly, one-fourth inch deep in rows twelve inches to fifteen inches apart. As lettuce matures, thin to eight inches to twelve inches between plants. (Thinnings can be transplanted to another row.) Water lettuce if the weather is warm. Harvest plants while leaves are tender.

Peppers

Peppers are warm seasoned and do best in a sunny, well-drained location. Like tomatoes, peppers produce best without too much nitrogen, so add compost in small amounts if the soil is already rich.

Start peppers indoors eight weeks ahead of setting out. Dig a large hole for adequate root spread. Partially fill, position pepper plant, fill in with remaining soil and firm. Water well and shade plants for several days to avoid shock.

Ah! The glorious summer garden! Ours lasts well into September, then ends with the return of cool evenings. Is this the end of our garden story? Hardly! Who says you have to wait 'til Spring?

CHAPTER 4

Who Says You Have to Wait 'Til Spring?

Few gardens can match the summer garden for variety, abundance and satisfaction. Depending on where you live, your summer gardening season may begin as early as February or March and extend through September. But does that mean you and your child must let the cooler months of the year go by? You needn't. Many gardeners are busy year-round.

Why Garden When It's Not Summer

Being outdoors in the tingling fall air, with its scent of woodsmoke and fluttering leaves, has a lot going for it. For me, fall is the best time of year. Canning season is complete. Jars rest on shelves full of the summer's harvest, that certain measure of self-sufficiency, the reward of a season's work. Still, the desire to plant and tend is there. Like the summer garden, the fall and winter garden has its promises too—fresh greens year-round when the stores have little to offer.

I'm not alone. For the kids, fall's crispy breezes revive the flagging feeling left from summer's end. For kids who enjoy school, it's a new beginning with exciting projects to come for a few months, anyway. It should be in your garden, too.

The fall garden offers your child a different gardening experience. If you compare warm season crops to cool season ones in your seed catalogs, you'll immediately notice the difference. Warm season vegetables offer fruits—eggplant, tomatoes, melons. Cool season vegetables, on the other hand, are leafy, like lettuce, spinach and mustard. In winter, it's the plant itself we eat: leaves, roots or flowers. Nutritionally, winter gardens pack in hefty servings of vitamins and minerals, unmatched by the summer fruits.

There's challenge in the successful fall garden—an interplay of timing, vegetable variety and weather, which spells the difference between success or failure. The time to plant part of your fall garden with your child is in the spring. Fall garden vegetables such as beets, cabbage and cauliflower require several months growing time to mature; therefore, they must be started early in the gardening year for a fall harvest.

Leafy vegetables such as spinach and mustard mature more quickly. They should be planted at the end of summer when the days are warm enough for fast germination, but not hot enough to cause the young plants to bolt, and the evening temperatures begin to dip. If your winters are harsh, choose quick maturing vegetables, ones which don't require much heat. Plan your harvest before the hard freezes.

What to Plant and How to Grow It

Some of the occupants of your winter garden should be those you grew as a first crop in your summer garden. Start radishes, carrots, lettuce, chard and onions while the daytime temperatures are still warm. With a couple of weeks of mild weather, these will be off to a good start. You'll find others your child may want to include in his or her fall garden. Like the summer vegetables, you should subject them to the "innocent-'til-proven-guilty" test, for winter vegetables must

Whether spring, summer, or fall, there's always something to do, something to learn in the garden.

earn their place in your child's garden, just as the summer vegetables do.

We don't consider some winter vegetables as "sure-fire" as others, so we try to plant ones the children like to eat. Spinach, contrary to popular myth, fixed in several winter casseroles, is one of the most asked for at our home. Depending on your children's tastes, here are some cool weather growers you can consider.

Fall and Winter Garden

Beets

A "two-for-the-price-of-one" vegetable, beets yield both tops and roots for eating. Colorwise, beets are great for a child's garden. The tops are green and red; the roots deep red or golden. Beets can be harvested first when half mature, or allowed to reach full size. Your child will be interested to know that the beet "seed" is not really just seed at all, but a tiny dried fruit, a natural package of beet seed.

Beets can be sown midsummer for a fall harvest. For faster germination have your child presoak the "seed" for 24 hours in compost water before planting.

Beets do best in friable, somewhat sandy soil, well worked with mature compost and limestone, if the soil is acid. Sow seed in prepared bed one inch deep in rows twelve inches apart. When plants are up, thin to four inches apart. Your child can transplant thinned seedlings to another row, if he wishes. Keep soil moist until seeds germinate.

Broccoli

I don't think I've ever met anyone who was uncommitted about broccoli—either you like it, or you don't. If your child likes its flavor, or is learning to like it, he or she should find it intriguing, since like cauliflower, it is one of few vegetables whose edible part is the blossom. Prove it by letting a few stalks mature. The broccoli flower is bright yellow and fragrant. Plant a few extra for color in your child's fall garden.

You can start broccoli from seed indoors several weeks before time to set out in midsummer, or you can buy starts from a nursery outlet, which is what we usually do.

For planting, choose a garden area with rich, well-drained soil. Transplant broccoli seedlings into a hole filled with a shovelful of mature, fine compost. Fill in with remaining soil and press firmly. Set young broccoli plants eighteen inches apart in rows twenty-four inches apart. Water well while the weather is warm.

Harvest broccoli by cutting the central head back when it is fully formed, but before it breaks open. After the center head is cut, smaller side heads will form and can be harvested at intervals.

Broccoli is hearty, and can be grown successfully until the first hard freeze. A light frost, in fact, improves its flavor.

Cabbage

For kids who like sauerkraut or cole slaw, here's the vegetable to grow. For winter contests it's a good choice, too. Some varieties reach twenty pounds. Cabbage in the fall garden is colorful—soft-hued greens and brilliant purples or reds.

Be sure to check dates to maturity on your seed packets before starting cabbage. Your first crop should be "early" and "midseason" varieties started indoors in flats, then transplanted when the ground is warm in the spring. "Medium early" cabbage can be started in cold frames or the ground. Start "late" cabbage directly in your child's permanent garden area.

Cabbage grows best in friable, moist soil with ample lime and lots of well-rotted manure. Sow cabbage seed a half-inch deep; cabbage plants should be placed three inches deep. Space early cabbage fifteen inches apart in rows; late cabbage should be spaced a little farther apart—up to twenty-four inches. Leave thirty inches between rows.

Cabbage plants have voracious appetites and dislike intense heat. During the dry summer months your child should keep them well watered to supply necessary nutrients. Shade them with newspaper or pieces of cardboard on hottest days. Cabbage is frequently attacked by garden pests, so you'll need to check plants. (For pest remedies, see chapter 5.)

When the cabbage head is fully formed, it can be harvested. Some gardeners force smaller heads of cabbage from early varieties by cutting the head, but leaving the plant in the ground. Occasionally, smaller heads will appear on side stalks. Your child may want to try forcing a second crop from the same plants.

Cauliflower

Another "flower" vegetable that has a special place in your child's fall garden is cauliflower. Its outer leaves are large, loose and green. From the center it produces its flower—a snowy-white, firm cluster, in most varieties. Probably, though, your child will want at least one purple-headed cauliflower, too. This vegetable is almost a snack food here. We serve it raw with dips, a nutritious alternative to potato chips and such.

We prefer to plant cauliflower from starts, but you can begin your own from seed in a cold frame, or sow seed directly into the ground midsummer. If you transplant, wait until plants are five weeks old, then move to the permanent garden area with rich soil in full sun. Cauliflower requires lots of compost, so use it generously.

Transplant seedlings leaving the rootball as undisturbed as possible. After your child's starts are planted, water liberally and mulch around the plant bases to conserve moisture and shade the roots.

As soon as your child notices the flower beginning to

Seeds.

Cabbage

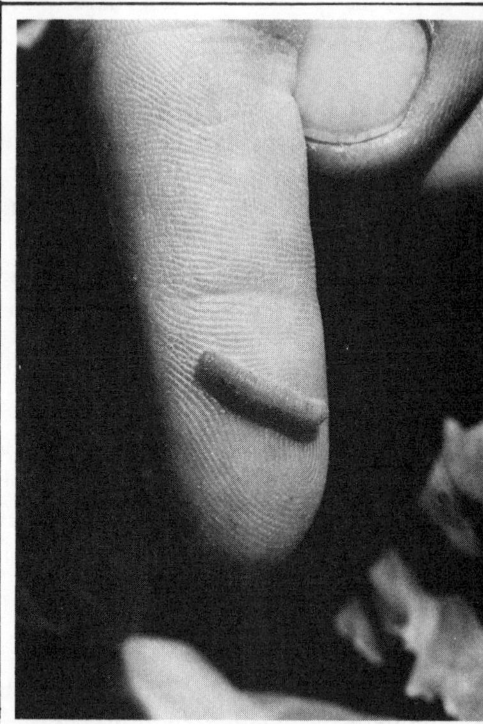

Cabbage looper.

The cabbage is an excellent vegetable to grow for contrast, for the difference between the size of the seed and the size of the ripe produce is remarkable. From seeds the size of BBs grow "heads" of cabbage as big as your head.

It takes a fairly long time, as vegetables go, so cabbage is usually started indoors. The initial sprouts give no clue as to the appearance of the final crop, a statement that's true of most, if not all, garden vegetables. Once the seedlings are established and the danger of frost is clearly past, the cabbages are moved outdoors and transplanted.

The main threat to the well-being of the cabbage is the cabbage looper, the offspring of the white cabbage moth. The moth, of

Seedling.

Headed out.

course, lays eggs that hatch out loopers. The loopers are so called because of the way their bodies hunch up into a loop as they inch along, rear end crowding up toward the front, then front moving away, then rear end crowding up again. The loopers feed on the cabbage plants—and all their relatives, like broccoli, cauliflower, and Brussels sprouts—until they enter the process that transforms them into moths.

Healthy cabbages growing in good fertile soil should survive the loopers, as well as other pests and diseases. Ultimately they will head out, forming great balls of tightly interlayered leaves.

form on his plants, they should not be exposed to sunlight. "Blanching" the heads makes them retain their white color and makes cauliflower more tender. To blanch, gather several large leaves around the head and tie them with a string or a rubber band. Leave the heads protected from the sun for eight to ten days—until the cauliflower head is fully formed and ready to eat.

Mustard

Since mustard is a food your child may often taste as a relish on hot dogs or hamburgers, growing it in his winter garden and eating it as a green might be a first time experience. A mainstay garden green prevalent in Southern Europe, we were introduced to it as children via my grandmother's extraordinary Italian kitchen, and have been hooked on it ever since. Boiled 'til limp, then gently sautéed in garlic and olive oil, mustard is a real taste change from usual winter vegetables. Many children, of course, won't care for this vegetable alone, but you can try it in casseroles, just as you would spinach or chard. Even if its taste doesn't turn your kids on, mustard is a fast grower and prolific, unlike other winter vegetables.

Mustard is definitely a cool weather crop. For the fall garden we plant ours in September, since an earlier planting will readily bolt in our intense valley heat. Plant in sandy soil worked with a small amount of mature compost. Sow seed a half-inch deep in rows twelve inches apart. When plants are up, thin to six inches. Thinnings can be used in salads.

Mustard is relatively disease free and generally easy to care for. Harvest, cutting the outer leaves when leaves reach six inches in height. Try to avoid letting mustard go to seed, as it will rapidly if not harvested. Ours did, and we fully expect an invasion of mustard plants in next year's spring garden!

Peas

Here's a vegetable designed for children if ever there was one in the fall garden. Rapidly growing on slender stalks with profusions of flowers, they're a change from the leafy green that predominates in the winter garden. Peas should be trained on poles, or staked—another winter garden project. The biggest thing going for them is that the majority of children enjoy their mild flavor and sweet taste. They're packaged too—shelling peas makes a good job for little kitchen helpers.

Snow or sugar peas should be included in your child's fall garden too. These peas have edible pods, which mean delicious eating without shelling. Try both varieties.

Your child's peas should be sown in the late summer for fall eating. Presoak seed, then plant three inches apart in double rows. Cover with one inch of soil lightly worked with mature compost. Peas, like beans, are nitrogen fixers if inoculated and do best in soil not overly rich. As soon as the young peas emerge, provide support for climbing varieties.

Begin to harvest sugar peas (edible pod) varieties when they are four inches long and before peas begin to bulge in the pod. Regular varieties should be picked when plump. Harvesting continually encourages heavy production.

Spinach

If your child will eat spinach, it's one of the best vegetables to command space in his winter garden. Full of vitamins and versatile in serving, spinach is one vegetable we always grow, except for the very hot summer months. Its leaves are a shiny green and slightly crinkled. For a different taste in salads, we like spinach raw with small pieces of bacon.

Spinach is another winter garden quick grower, which does best in a cool garden location. A heavy nitrogen user, spinach grows well in soil heavily worked with mature compost. Plant spinach seed a half-inch deep, three to four

Seeds.

Peas

Peas are the vegetables you sample right there in the garden. The sugars that make them so sweet and tasty as you chew them standing in the garden start changing to starches when you pick the peas. And the starches are less sweet and tasty. Like corn, you've got to eat peas straight from the harvest for the very best flavor.

With the exception of sugar peas or snow peas, which are grown for the edible pods, peas are cultivated for the seeds, those familiar green tidbits. The seeds are sown directly in the garden, and for best results, they should be inoculated with a special bacteria just before the seeds are put in the ground. Together, plant and bacteria can pull nitrogen, a vital plant nutrient, right out of the air, something neither plant nor bacteria alone can do. And only plants whose fruits are pods—the plants are called legumes—can do it, even if inoculated.

Peas are viney plants, and they develop interesting tendrils that will entwine anything they touch, including other tendrils. Consequently, peas should be

Blossoms.

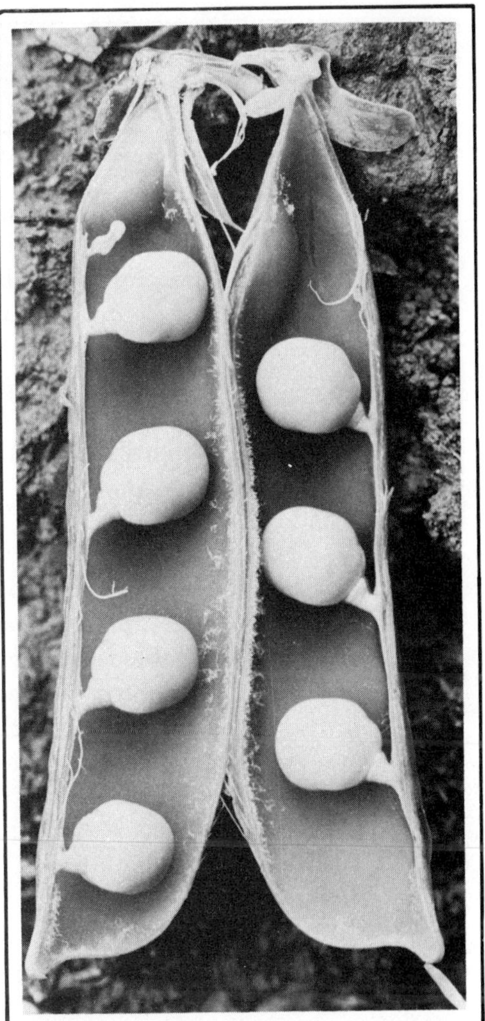

Seven peas in a pod.

Harvest.

trellised for ease of harvesting: they'll climb up a section of chicken-wire fence and display the pea pods for you, or they'll hide the pods in a tangle of vines on the ground.

After the blossoms come the pods, which slowly expand to accommodate the growing peas. If you've got sugar peas, be sure to pick the pods before the peas develop or the pods will be too tough to taste good. If you've got peas in mind, let 'em fill the pods before picking.

inches apart in rows twelve inches apart. Your child should plan an August planting if your weather is not too hot, or wait until the first week of September when evening temperatures begin to fall, and days are not too hot. Spinach can be harvested like chard. Have your child remove only the outer leaves, leaving the smaller inner leaves to mature. Spinach, by the way, can be wintered over with adequate protection, making for early spring greens.

Crops That Will Winter Over

Several vegetables in your child's fall/winter garden can successfully be grown through the winter months. Your child's garden in a mild climate can be a real success story, supplying vegetables well into December, if you prepare carefully. By the time temperatures begin to rise in the spring, your son's or daughter's cool weather crops will be off to a fine start—already *in* the garden and ready to grow. Wintered over vegetables are practically guaranteed to be the first to the table in the spring. If they're your child's vegetables, so much the better. You can be tasting your first garden greens as the seed catalogs arrive—double incentive to plan the greatest garden ever for the following year. Finally, the wintered over garden, once prepared, takes little care. That leaves you free for other projects.

Just what do I mean by "wintering over?" Which vegetables are likely candidates for a fast spring start?

The answer to these two questions will depend somewhat on where you live. Here, we have successfully wintered over Swiss chard, spinach, mustard, carrots, onions and strawberries (a perennial). Since our ground doesn't freeze, digging root crops for winter use isn't a problem. In severe climates it would be.

In wintering over the kids' garden, we set a very simple goal. Keep the vegetables alive and healthy enough to give them a good start in the spring. That's it. But it's enough. Here's why.

If your child begins to winter over with the expectation of being able to harvest from his garden year-round, he may be in for a disappointment. In an area like ours, sometimes a garden will actually produce through December and sometimes it won't. Therefore, we seek "success" in the spring from our vegetables off to an early start, *not* during the coldest months. Of course, if winter is mild, and we can eat from our gardens through the coldest months, great! But we never plan on it, so we aren't disappointed.

Once your child decides he would like to winter over part of his garden, where should you begin?

Start by culling all but the healthiest cool weather plants at the end of the harvest season. Next, plan a general clean-up. Put fallen leaves into the compost pile along with weeds that may have cropped up during the busy harvest season. Check your plants for pests, and if you find them, get them under control.

Now you're ready to prepare your plants for survival. What do they need? Everything they do during the growing season plus protection from the cold.

After removing any weeds and checking for pests, we cultivate around each plant lightly, then cover the entire root area up to the stems with a mature compost layer from one to three inches thick, depending on the height of the plant. Over this layer we spread a thick layer of cut straw. Leafy vegetables we cover right up to the bottom leaves. Next comes water, and that's it—the kids' garden is put to bed for the winter, except for an occasional watering.

If you need protection from snow, build your mulch layer several inches over the entire plants. In a "hard freeze" climate without snow, mulch, then use inverted jars for protection on coldest nights.

Another method we've had good luck with, when the night temperatures threaten to dip into the 20s, is to water spray the garden lightly. The moisture left on the plant leaves by a fine spray freezes at 32 degrees, protecting the plant from freeze burn and dehydration from lower temperatures. Just be sure to use a fine spray, since too much water will cause the stems to break from weight.

Another way to protect your child's vegetables from the ravages of winter is simply to move them to a cold frame, a greenhouse or indoors. Leafy vegetables such as lettuce and spinach will survive in a cold frame under the eaves, or in a garage or shed near a light source. One caution here, though. Be sure your child checks for water—especially when it's rainy. We've lost plants from drying out under the eaves during a long storm. We didn't think to water them.

Tender Lovin' Care for Winter Gardens

Once your child's vegetables are snugly prepared for slumber during the winter months, is your fall gardening complete? No, not quite, because a winter garden, to our way of thinking, is a garden in preparation. Next season, after all, is only two or three months off. What we do now is important to next year's success.

What's there to do? Last summer's vegetables which are still in the ground should be picked and stored—tomatoes, eggplant, squash, cucumbers, peppers, pumpkins, sunflowers. Eggplant, peppers and tomatoes should be uprooted entirely and hung upside down so that their fruits finish maturing. Winter squash should be picked, stored for several weeks in a warm place, then moved to cold storage.

Remaining stalks and plants should be gathered up, shredded and placed in the compost pile. We then turn the garden area under, checking for insect hideouts, plant root diseases, or other potential garden trouble spots. These disposed of, we spread a two by three inch layer of manure over the entire garden.

Next, it's time to check garden equipment and make repairs. Check tool handles and implement edges, watching especially for splinters and chips. Power equipment we clean, check for oil changes and general maintenance. On to the cold frames next to check for broken slats, missing nails and weather-beaten plastic. Usually, the end of the garden season means storage areas need straightening, since we're not too neat. Last of all, we gather our remaining seed packets, putting each type seed in a container with a snug lid. These we label and store in a cool, dry place for next year.

Thus our outdoor gardening season officially ends. Our children's wintered over vegetables are ready for their fast spring start; the garden area rests in preparation for next year.

The summer garden, the winter garden. Each in its own way is a different gardening experience for your child. Next, let's look at keeping your gardens at their best by beating the bugs and other stuff.

CHAPTER 5

Beating the Bugs and Other Stuff

Challenge. A call to the full use of our abilities. For your child, as for all organic gardeners, the challenge is to grow healthy vegetables—those which aren't plagued by disease and pests, then doused with chemicals which threaten the quality of our lives and the food we bring to our tables.

Over the years, careful observation of what goes on in the garden, and use of research into the nature of plant infestations and disease, has expanded our knowledge about potential garden problems. The trial and error methods of thousands of gardeners who prefer ingenuity to poisons have proven it is possible to have a thriving garden without these substances.

Starting the sure-fire garden with vegetables your child has chosen—ones tasting good, and fun to grow, is only the beginning of the successful gardening experience. Most of all your child's garden should be a happy place—and a safe one. It's time to think about garden safety, garden care, companion planting, and safe, sane pest control.

Keeping Your Child's Garden Safe

What makes a child's garden safe or unsafe will be very much related to his age and personality. Children learn caution as they grow older; some children are cautious by nature. You may have one child you rarely worry about and another who precipitates a yearly trip to the emergency room. If your children are young, you'll be exercising extra vigilance in the garden as you would in any outdoor activity.

The first potential garden hazard has already been mentioned—garden tools. Providing your child learns to use them properly and has an adequate tool to do the job at hand, the only other danger that comes to mind is the hazard invited by tools left lying around. Rakes left tines-up on the ground invite puncture wounds and a good smack in the head if stepped on. Weed pullers in the hands of a child tearing across the backyard can be as lethal as falling on a knife or pair of scissors. Improperly stored tools will weather, resulting in rusty cuts and splinters. Any of these dangers can be avoided by proper storage after gardening and *during* gardening. Power tools must be used correctly to prevent injury to those using them, and for those nearby.

Another danger in the emergency room category we constantly watch for is ingestion of harmful substances. You've already eliminated a tremendous worry by not using chemicals in your garden. Watch out, though, for seemingly innocuous substances—seeds, for example, which have been chemically treated with fungicides.

Since you and your child will probably spend a good deal of time outdoors, now is as good a time as any to check your immediate area for poisonous plants. The castor plant is a good example. It grows wild and is grown as an ornamental and as an agricultural crop. Both the seeds and foliage of young seedlings are highly poisonous. Two or three seeds can kill a child—six seeds, an adult.

The oleander is a flowery evergreen shrub, popular because of its beauty and tolerance to wet and dry extremes. It is often used as a barrier hedge. All parts of this plant are poisonous, even dried up fallen leaves. Smoke from burning oleander can make some people ill, so take precaution if you dispose of it.

Organic plant protection: A praying mantis, a companion planting, a preying gardene

Other particularly poisonous plants which can invade the garden area are toadstools, which grow abundantly in manure, poison oak or ivy, poison hemlock, black nightshade, tree tobacco and mistletoe.

Plants containing one or more poisonous parts often used in a landscape design include, but aren't limited to, monkshood, Bushman's poison, belladonna lily, autumn crocus, meadow saffron, lily-of-the valley, daphne, larkspur, delphinium, foxglove, golden chain, ngaio, narcissus, daffodil and pittosporum.

Beware also of bites and stings. A small child who steps onto a large ant hill can be severely harmed if not helped right away. Several beestings can make a baby quite ill and severely harm any child or adult who is allergic to bee venom. Garden spiders are usually harmless, but we watch for black widows in the wood pile, and centipedes which are numerous in our area. Because we live in a rural area, we have snakes to contend with. So far we've found only four harmless garter or king snakes, but a diamond-back rattler wouldn't be a surprise. Johnny is instructed to call us immediately if he sees (or hears!) any snake.

Trapped or injured animals—rabbits, gophers, moles, ground squirrels, raccoons—will bite a child if he gets too close, and some of these can carry rabies, or may be infested with fleas carrying bubonic plague.

Living in the city doesn't always mean immunity from possible dangers. I know a preschooler left with a lacerated scalp when he was attacked in his front yard by an angry bluejay. Rare occurrences, yes, but such things do happen. Accidents are by their very nature unexpected.

Garden Care

Lack of good garden care is probably responsible for more garden failure than any other reason. Vegetable plants which must compete for light, air, moisture and nutrients with each other or weeds will be stunted and lack vigor.

Your goal should be a garden full of healthy plants in tiptop shape, able to withstand normal perils like insect attacks and adverse weather changes.

Thinning

It's tough to uproot healthy plants, but thinning is absolutely necessary for vigorous garden growth. Thinning is simply pulling up plants in an area where they are too crowded, to get the best possible spacing for maximum growth.

You probably won't have to thin your child's corn, beans, onions, melons or cucumbers, squash, eggplant, tomatoes or peppers, since some will be transplanted from your hotbed or cold frame and can be properly spaced at the time. Others have seed large enough to allow your child to space them out while sowing. The small seeded vegetables, though, will probably need thinning.

Your child should thin his rows when seedlings first begin to crowd up. Bunched seedlings invite damping off. For easier thinning, choose a time when the soil is moist. Tweezers work quite well on slender seedlings. Root crops such as carrots should be thinned before the root has a chance to thicken. That way you won't be disrupting carrots you want to remain. For leafy crops, we generally use a first, second and third thinning system. Crowded seedlings are removed right away. Then when the plants are large enough to use in salads, but long before they're mature, we thin to the distance recommended for whichever vegetable we're taking care of. Swiss chard is a good example. We sow, thin first to separate seedlings, then thin to three inches apart. When the leaves begin to touch one another, we pull up every other plant, eventually leaving the chard at six inch intervals. From these plants we harvest the outer leaves all through the season.

Watering

Another big item in determining a garden's success or failure is how you and your child water his garden.

Water is absolutely essential to all life, for a number of reasons. In the case of plants, it is a primary source of the hydrogen used in the manufacture of plant food. Water also serves as a vehicle which carries essential soluble minerals from the soil to the plant leaves.

How much water a vegetable receives at a particular time is very important, first of all for plant survival, and second, for good yield. *How* we water, therefore, changes somewhat as our garden progresses through the season.

In the beginning, before your seed has germinated, it must not be allowed to dry out. In our garden, if seeds fail to sprout, lack of water is usually the reason.

During normal plant growth after germination you should try to water according to a particular plant's requirements. Remember, tomatoes, for instance, require much less water than corn.

We've found that following some general tips greatly increase the chances of using water to maximum benefit.

Encourage your child to water more *thoroughly* than frequently. Light sprinklings will not produce deep-rooted, vigorous plants. Soak the garden to a depth of six inches, then don't water again until the first half-inch to one inch of soil has dried out. Why? Simply because two things can't be in the same space at the same time. In this case, air and water. Plants need both.

If your child's garden is continually wet, it is impossible for the oxygen-carbon dioxide exchange to take place at the plant root. Your child's vegetables won't survive waterlogged conditions. Too much water will also cause the valuable soil nutrients you've worked hard to get into the soil to leach out.

On the other hand, your vegetables shouldn't be allowed to dry out. Plants suffering from water stress expend much hard-gotten energy just trying to recover when they should be producing bountiful crops.

How can your child tell if his vegetables are getting enough, but not too much water? The best way is to check with a trowel for soil moisture. If the soil is barely damp an inch down it's probably time for your child to water. The condition of his plants tells a lot too. Beans deprived of water will turn yellow, and the pods will shrivel. Radishes will be hot, small and pithy. Cucumbers will be soft instead of plump, cool and firm.

Yield is very much affected by ample amounts of water. In general we don't get too scientific about it, but try, never-the-less, to maintain a reasonable water program in both ours and our children's gardens. We add more water than usual when vegetables are just nearing harvest—it seems to increase our yield.

Besides the amount of water you use, the time you choose to water can affect the vegetables your child grows. Here, in the cooler spring and fall, we try to water in the morning. In the summer heat, we switch to evening watering. That way we lose less moisture to evaporation and prevent sun scald on the wet foliage. Wet foliage can cause plant disease to spread more rapidly, if you have infected plants. If you do choose evening watering, allow enough time for the plants to dry out before nightfall, and avoid handling the wet plants, for risk of carrying infection to healthy plants.

Since your child's garden isn't terribly large, just use a hose, with or without a nozzle, a watering can, or a sprinkler set in the center of the garden. Older children who've really taken to large-scale gardening should look into simple irrigation systems.

Cultivation

I remember a time when we didn't weed our garden. Our vegetables started off just fine, then suddenly quit. The garden was a total bust. I really wondered why—after all, the weeds seemed to flourish with the vegetables; why didn't our vegetables flourish with the weeds?

Among other things, I'd guess it's partly a case of sheer numbers. There are innumerable weeds which grow quite nicely under adverse conditions—most vegetables won't. Conditions suitable for vegetables are just fantastic for weeds—plenty of food, light, water, how can they lose? Beyond that it's a case of out-stripping. Weeds don't really become a problem until they threaten to take over. Unfortunately that may be only a matter of a week. Vegetables just can't beat the weed's accelerated timetable.

Then too, definitions are part of the problem. A weed in its loosest sense is *any* plant that doesn't belong in our vegetable garden—like the mustard we inadvertently let go to seed last season. It will turn up elsewhere in the garden, probably in the wrong place next year. In short, last year's winter crop will become next spring's weed.

So why are weeds so awful, anyway? First of all, weeds rob the soil of moisture which vegetables need to grow. They begin to shade vegetable plants, and soon their ambitious root systems are in direct competition for soil nutrients. The unhappy truth is, weeds in your child's garden will cause his vegetables to starve to death!

One answer to the weed problem is cultivation—simply removing the weeds from your child's garden early and as often as necessary to maintain vigorous growth of the vegetables he has planted. The easiest way to weed a small garden is to pick a few each night, or in the morning while the ground is moist.

If your child's garden is good sized, a hoe will do the job nicely. Your son or daughter can chop through the weed roots a few inches below the soil surface, just taking care not to come too close to the plants in order not to disturb the vegetable roots. Those in between the plants can be hand pulled.

Hoeing this way also aerates the soil by breaking up any hard crust that may have formed as a result of rain or irrigation.

Miracle Worker—Mulch

Mulching your child's garden is an even better way to beat the weeds. The hoed down weeds themselves make a good mulch layer providing they haven't gone to seed. Just allow them to lay underneath the vegetables once they've been uprooted. Add to them any grass clippings or raked leaves you have. If you come up short of mulching materials, look around for likely sources. In our area we can get wood chips, rice hulls and sawdust with no problem at all. Straw we use frequently. We buy in bales from local feed stores. If we were desperate for mulching material, that pile of newspapers cluttering up the garage would work very well. Black plastic is another possibility, which we normally rule out because of expense and availability of other materials. But if your child's garden is not too large, you might consider it.

What is it that mulch does that makes it popular with organic gardeners? First of all, a thick mulch layer prevents rapid moisture evaporation from the soil surface. Second, as it decomposes and is worked into the ground, it adds to the soil humus content and thereby substantially improves the soil's moisture-holding qualities. In soil which has a tendency to become waterlogged, extra humus over the years will break up hard layers, making for better drainage. In sandy soils or soils with lots of gravel, the mulching material will absorb water and tend to hold it from draining away too rapidly.

What about weeds, though? What does mulch do for them? For one thing, mulch shades the ground so effectively that many weed seeds simply don't germinate. Those that do can be easily spotted and picked out by hand. If there is a miracle worker that goes hand in hand with cultivation for your child's garden—and your own—it's got to be mulch!

Making Friends—Companion Plants for Your Child's Garden

The preference of some plants for other plants, and similarly, the dislike of certain plants for others has been widely documented, but so far not thoroughly researched. Yet companion planting—putting certain plants near ones they seem to like—is one of the best "green thumb" secrets to a really successful garden. As your children's gardening interests expand, they'll probably be very interested in experimenting with companion plants.

Over the years, organic gardeners have been aware that, planted together, certain plants seem to benefit each other. For example, beans seem to help corn, and peppers do well planted near tomatoes. On the other hand, mature dill for some unknown reason retards the growth of carrots and tomatoes!

How all of this works is not entirely understood. Beans and other legumes probably benefit vegetables planted near them because of the increased nitrogen they add to the soil. For heavy nitrogen users, like corn, the amount of nitrogen made available by the legumes helps supply their hefty appetites.

Proper shading is another probable answer. Taller plants will shade smaller ones some time during the day—lettuce planted next to radishes, for example.

It's also been discovered that all plants excrete chemicals called "root diffusates." Root diffusates affect plants growing near them in a way that is not understood. But the benefits have been observed. Certain vegetables really "turn on" when others are around—they grow faster, larger and tastier. You've got the right to be skeptical, of course, but that's part of the gardening challenge—finding the combinations that work for you in your garden. You can begin with these combinations, then try your own:

Beans with corn, carrots, cucumbers, radishes, but not with onions or sunflowers.
Parsley with onions, carrots, corn, tomatoes
Carrots with lettuce, radishes, peas, cucumbers, beans
Corn with cucumbers, melons, squash, beans, peas, pumpkins
Cucumbers with corn, lettuce, beans, radishes
Lettuce with onions, radishes
Peppers with tomatoes, eggplant, onions
Radishes with pole beans, leaf lettuce
Soybeans with corn
Basil with lettuce
Chives with carrots and tomatoes
Summer Savory with onions, beans
Eggplant with beans, peppers

Fortunately, the happy story of companion planting doesn't end here. While your companion plants are turning on to each other, they're *turning off* the bugs. Skeptics take note!

One sound explanation has to do with intercropping—the practice of planting more than one crop in a large area. In countries where mechanized farming isn't large scale, farmers have found their insect population cut by fifty percent when they avoid planting fields with just one crop. Why? Because insects are attracted by chemicals, colors, movement, or other characteristics of plants. The more there is of one type of vegetable in an area, the more powerful the signal to insect predators. *That* makes sense. And what's more, the more food available, the longer insects are wont to stay around before moving on.

The small home gardener is already at an advantage, because he grows a variety of crops. Add companion planting—several vegetable types even within one row, and insects have a hard time zeroing in.

Have we reached the end of the companion planting story? Not quite.

Not only does intercropping discourage insect attack by limiting attraction to a certain area, but some plants deter insects from attacking certain other plants they like. It's probably a case of the bees in the honey tree—is the honey worth the risk? An aphid has to "decide" whether that choice morsel is worth getting near the garlic plants. If the garlic wins out even one quarter of the time, companion planting has paid off!

Here are some plants reputed to deter common garden insects:

Garlic and onions repel aphids, mosquitoes, caterpillars, sucking insects.
Marigolds repel nematodes, whitefly, bean beetles.
Nasturtiums repel squash bugs.
Rosemary repels carrot fly.
Mint repels ants.
Sage repels cabbage worm butterfly.

Remembering that companion planting isn't an exact science, you and your child might experiment with these plants—largely herbs, which are said to be generally beneficial to practically all garden vegetables: dill except with carrots and tomatoes; garlic except near beans or peas; chives, generally good, especially with carrots and tomatoes; sweet marjoram, oregano, rosemary, sage, tarragon, thyme; mint, which improves the flavor of tomatoes; and for protection against the bugs, basil, anise and coriander.

Moving On—Crop Rotation

Every gardener will be bothered from time to time with plant disease. They may be viral or fungal infections, or a host of pathogenic bacteria which plant pathologists know much better than the average home gardener. Still, much of disease treatment is prevention in the first place. How you and your children plan your garden from season to season can cut down on these problems before they begin—or prevent them from recurring the next year. In short, it's simply a matter of growing the healthiest plants possible, and limiting environments where diseases thrive.

We've already talked about choosing varieties that are resistant to common diseases—planting tomatoes resistant to fusarium wilt, for example. Beyond that, moving vegetables from one place to another each season will really cut down on disease for two reasons.

First, all vegetables use soil nutrients in different amounts. Some vegetables will take much more potassium from the soil than others—root crops such as carrots are an example. If your child grows his carrots in the same place from year to year, the potassium levels can drop severely, the result being sickly carrots that are much less likely to resist disease than those that are vigorous. Corn extracts large amounts of nitrogen from the soil. Grown year after year in the same place, it will soon deplete the soil, and stalks will become stunted and subject to corn diseases. Even when you're adding organic fertilizers to your soil each year, as you should, rotating the crops evens out soil depletion and gives each area of your garden a chance to build up—not just keep even—with the nutritional demands of the vegetables grown in it.

Second, by rotating your crops from season to season, your child can avoid adding fuel to the fire if a disease should invade. Since disease is caused by living organisms, their survival depends on favorable conditions. If you, in effect, "feed" them their favorite vegetable year after year, they'll multiply, causing widespread damage. Crop rotation, in many instances, cuts off the supply. Nematodes on tomato roots can be discouraged simply by planting disease-free tomatoes in a different area from year to year.

Finally, diseased plants should be removed from the garden and burned. Don't turn them into the garden.

Putting Up with Pests—Control vs. Eradication

In your child's garden, or any organic garden for that matter, how much the bugs bug you will be largely a matter of attitude. I'll give you an example. In our garden we don't try to wipe out every tomato horn worm tempted to take up residence. Instead of spraying and spraying, if they become a problem, we pick them off by hand. The result is a few chewed leaves, granted. And at first this bothered us. Then we learned a few interesting things about pests.

Fact number one. Studies have shown that some crops can lose up to thirty percent of their leaf mass, without *any* decrease in yield! That says a lot. It's a primary argument against those who complain that organic methods don't work—they don't get rid of the bugs. What we reminded ourselves is that those who insist they must use chemical means of pest control arm themselves with an arsenal of chemicals and wage a war of eradication. Unfortunately, the chemical systems often destroy the good bugs as well as the bad, compounding pest problems in the following years, not to mention the pollution they cause. For goodness sakes, why? Good pest control (not eradication) can yield the same crop and at what environmental savings!

And if that's not enough to favor sensible pest control methods, we've learned something even more fascinating. Fact number two. Some plants actually benefit from insect attacks! Hard to believe? Well, the effect isn't much different from pruning—if an insect chews off the terminal bud of a plant, it encourages new shoots. In addition, insect damage to some plants can result in the stimulation of beneficial plant hormones.

This is not to say that pests in the garden aren't a problem. They can be. But as organic gardeners we believe in the balances of the ecosystem—gardening with the least disturbance to the environment, and using nature's means for pest control if things get out of hand, such as introducing biocontrols instead of chemicals into the garden when pests or disease become a problem. To our way of thinking, a few chewed leaves now and then is much more livable than a garden sprayed and dusted with noxious substances for a problem that might not even occur.

Many potential garden problems can be prevented simply by providing an environment favorable to birds and insects that prey on those who have an appetite for your vegetables. Birds are frequently overlooked in a garden scheme. Voracious insect eaters that they are, they shouldn't be. This year we've begun planting our total yard with the birds in mind. In exchange for the food, water, shelter and nesting materials we'll be offering, they'll probably go a long way to reduce what insect garden problems we anticipate. And birds are fascinating garden companions in and of themselves. If your child is interested in attracting birds to his garden, see chapter 7.

Garden Housekeeping

Besides the right attitude, the next step to keep the bugs from bugging you is to begin rigorous garden housekeeping.

We've been discouraged from time to time to find a newly sprouted row of lettuce totally mowed down in one night by an insect we couldn't spot. Insects, like the rest of us, prefer those places where they're most comfortable. They may live in one place and forage in another—your child's garden.

What can you do about elusive maurauders? First of all, determine what's causing the damage. Look for telltale signs—chewed leaves, curled leaves, slime trails, droppings, egg clusters, etc. Anything unusual seeming to cause damage to some plants, maybe not all of them, could be your early warning of an insect invasion.

Even if you can't find them, look for favorite hiding places. We've found sow bug colonies under piles of straw, earwigs by the dozens in discarded newspapers, slugs and snails under old pieces of lumber and bricks, ants gathered around fallen fruit. Insects, many of them harmful, will flock to a sloppy garden. If you're unwittingly extending open house to pests by what's around your child's garden area, straighten up.

If your garden housekeeping is completed and you're still bothered by pests, identification is important. We try to spot the culprit—usually by observing the vegetable several times a day over a period of several days. Not an all-out hunt, just a *look* from time to time. If there is enough of an infestation to worry about, it won't take you and your child long to find what's causing the damage. Next, we look through the literature we've collected—most of it from the agricultural department of the county for minimal cost—and compare the bug to the photos of pests most likely to attack that particular vegetable. Nine times out of ten, it's one of those. From there, we turn to resource material on which method of pest control to use.

Supersafe Methods of Pest Control

Some insects invading your child's garden will be easy to spot, large and slow moving enough to be picked off by hand. Tomato horn worms most readily come to mind. We just pluck them from the vine and destroy them.

Besides hand elimination, another simple, fast, perfectly safe way of ridding your child's garden of unbidden guests is to spray them away with water. This method works particularly well for aphids. During much of their complicated life cycle aphids are unable to fly, and once knocked off a plant, stay off. The winged ones may alight again, but we've found a daily spraying eliminates most of our aphid problem.

For many gardeners, good old soap and water is an effective treatment for aphids that persist after the water treatments. Dissolve 3 tablespoons soap (such as Ivory, a nondetergent) into a gallon of water and apply with a spray can. The soap solution won't harm your child's vegetables, and it will discourage aphids.

Snails, slugs and earwigs (pincher bugs) can ravage a garden in one free-for-all evening, unless you and your child plan an ambush. Snails and slugs both can be foiled by an ingeniously simple method. Your child can sink the tops of margarine lids, or a similar container into the ground so that the rim is even with the soil surface. Then just fill the container with beer. In the morning, you'll find quite a few snails and slugs safely drowned. The treatment for earwigs is just as simple. Make the critters comfortable. Roll up some newspapers and leave them around your garden area. In the morning, burn them without unrolling them and voilà—no more earwigs.

In similar manner, you can control maggots affecting root crops by sprinkling wood ash around the plant base. Stem borers can be eliminated by locating the point of entry, slitting the stem with a sharp knife, and destroying the offender.

Ladybug, Ladybug— Natural Predators Your Child Will Love

One of the largest problems with widespread use of chemical pesticides is that these noxious substances are largely nonselective—they kill off good bugs as well as bad. Many commercial farmers who have used pesticides find their infestations increased in the years following spraying because they have eradicated those insects that would normally help keep pest populations under control. As a result, commercial farmers are reintroducing insects that have been wiped out by indiscriminate spraying.

By not using chemicals in your child's garden, you'll be taking the first step towards maintaining natural ecological balance. If one pest becomes a problem, which may occasionally happen, you and your child can easily duplicate nature's balance with natural predators like ladybugs (also called lady beetles), praying mantises and lacewings.

Ladybugs are usually abundant when aphids appear in the spring. The adult ladybug your child should already know—plump, black headed, with bright orange wings, some spotted black. The larvae of ladybugs your child may not recognize as readily—slender and wingless, black bodied with orange spots. In cooler temperatures, the adults hibernate after mating. The warm weather which brings out aphids in numbers is their cue to reawaken and lay the eggs they have been carrying since the previous year. Ladybug larvae have an enormous appetite for many types of soft-bodied insects including aphids and thrips. Introduced to your child's garden, they will remain as long as the food supply is plentiful. When food dwindles ladybugs will move on, but not before having polished off a large number of your child's garden pests.

Ladybugs are becoming so popular you may be able to buy them in a local nursery outlet. (We bought 2,000 this year from a local drugstore that has a garden department.) The appendix lists ladybug suppliers from whom you can order if you can't find them locally.

The praying mantis is a natural predator, like the ladybug, which does a bang-up job of eliminating garden pests. The praying mantis is a long-legged insect with large antennae and forelegs that fold, making the insect look as if it's praying. They're large, but sometimes hard to spot since their color blends with its surroundings, and they'll be perfectly still when they sense danger.

The young mantises particularly relish aphids and flies; adult mantises have a taste for beetles, caterpillars, and grasshoppers. They are supplied in "egg cases," each of which will hatch out about 300 baby mantises. Your child can tie the cases suspended in a small mesh bag to a tree or another garden plant. Mantises can usually be purchased from the same outlets that carry ladybugs. Both mantises and ladybugs should be stored in the refrigerator if you aren't going to release them right away.

The lacewing fly is a small insect with a voracious appetite for aphids. Your child will like its soft, almost iridescent green color, and patterned wings that look much like the veins of leaves, a lacy effect from which the lacewing gets its name. Lacewings, at least here, are not yet a nursery item, but you can order from suppliers. Some are listed in the appendix. They can also be raised at home, an interesting project for school-aged children or groups of children.

Organic Insecticides and Traps— Is There a Place for Them in Your Child's Garden?

In almost any organic family garden, naturally derived insecticides have a place from time to time. These dusts or sprays including *Bacillus thuringiensis*, pyrethrum, rotenone and ryania, are considered by many organic gardeners as a last-ditch defense to be used only when an infestation threatens to destroy a vegetable and other means of control aren't adequate.

Bacillus thuringiensis, sold commercially as Thuricide and Biotrol, is a dust of live spores that cause disease in certain insects, thereby eliminating them. B.T. is helpful in controlling cabbage loopers and cabbage worms. It is readily decomposed by organisms living in the soil.

Pyrethrum is an insecticide found in the flowers of a type of chrysanthemum. Usually supplied as a dust for home garden use, it works by contact and as a stomach poison, paralyzing insects. Pyrethrum is a powerful insecticide, but easily broken down by sunlight, leaving no harmful residue. It is effective against aphids, Mexican bean beetles, cabbage worms, thrips, loopers, leafhoppers, and others. It is not compatible with soaps.

Rotenone is an insecticide that comes from the derris root, a plant native to South America. Slow acting, rotenone works by contact and as a stomach poison by inhibiting oxygen use by the insects' body cells. It is useful for controlling pests on bush crops, beans, corn, eggplant, mustard, peas, radishes, strawberries, tomatoes and other vegetables. It controls beetles, slugs, loopers, cabbage worms, thrips. Rotenone is usually supplied as a one-half to one percent dust or four to five percent wettable powder. Rotenone should not be used with lime. Its effects last about a week, after which rotenone is rendered harmless by oxygen and sunlight.

Ryania is another slow acting insecticide that causes insects to quit eating. Sold under the trade name Ryanicide, it is derived from the stem of a shrub native to the Amazon Basin, and sold as a fifty percent wettable powder, which is used as a spray. It is effective against corn earworms, aphids, leafhoppers, onion thrips, some beetles, and squash bugs.

How do these insecticides come to be accepted by organic gardeners? Each is derived from a biological source—a microorganism, or plant, and unlike hard chemicals, have no deleterious effect on the environment. They are short acting and easily broken down by natural processes.

The question, though, is are they safe for use in your child's garden? That's hard to answer with a rigid yes or no, since the best answer is your own—knowing your procedures for protecting your children from harmful household materials, knowing your own child and the condition of his garden. Are more powerful pest control methods necessary for its success?

Hopefully the following information will help you decide whether you wish to use these biological and botanical insecticides in your child's garden.

Thuricide is not toxic to animals and presumably can be used safely. Pyrethrum has a lethal dose of 200 milligrams per kilogram. In simple terms, a half teaspoon of *pure* pyrethrum can cause death for a child weighing 30 pounds. Rotenone has a lethal dose of 132 mg/kg—¼ teaspoon to 30 pounds. Ryania rates in toxicity at 1200 mg/kg—3 teaspoons per 30 pounds.

While the figures above look ominous, toxicity depends very much on the percentage of pure compound in any actual preparation. Checking the active ingredients listed on a one-pound container of a combination organic insecticide which is available commercially, I find:

Pyrethrins	0.100%
Rotenone	0.750%
Other cube resins	1.500%
Ryanodine	0.055%
Inert ingredients	97.595%

A child would probably have to swallow a substantial amount of this particular mixture to ingest a lethal dose of any one ingredient. However, it could conceivably happen. The other point to bear in mind is that the percentages these compounds are supplied in varies greatly—ryania most often comes as a fifty percent wettable powder. Inert ingredients shouldn't be ignored either—they aren't listed, so there is no way to determine their toxicity.

The list mentioned above was taken from a can of organic insecticide we have used in our family garden. We therefore have it stored around the house—out of the reach of the children.

We have not so far used any pesticides in the children's garden. Whether we will depends on whether or not an infestation is really severe—enough *to make something fail*, if other safer methods don't work.

The same thinking applies to traps commonly used to control rodents and small animals. We have used traps for rabbits—one Johnny and his father built, which is perfectly safe and allowed us to release the cottontails unharmed a mile or so away from the garden. We have used commercially available traps designed for gophers, which kill them. In selecting ones we thought would be the safest for use in the

BEATING THE BUGS

Vegetable	Symptoms
Beans	Clusters of insects on leaves
	Round holes in leaves
	Plants eaten off at ground level during the night
	Hopping insects on leaves
	Leaves eaten between veins
	Small white insects which flutter when vegetable is shaken
Beets	Leaves chewed; slime trails
Broccoli	Clusters of insects on leaves
	Maggots on roots; plant doesn't look healthy
	Holes eaten in leaves
	Plants eaten off at ground level at night
Cabbage	Clusters of small insects on leaves
	Maggots on roots; plant doesn't look healthy
	Holes eaten in leaves
	Plants eaten off at ground level at night
Carrots	Tunneled by larvae
Cauliflower	Clusters of small insects on leaves
	Maggots on roots; plant doesn't look healthy
	Holes eaten in leaves

est	*Hand remove*	*Water spray*	*Soap spray*	*Place collar around stem and into soil*	*Use beer containers*	*Put out rolled newspapers*	*Slit stem; destroy bug*	*Sprinkle wood ash around plant*	*Rotate crop*	*Use Thuricide*	*Use Pyrethrum*	*Use Rotenone*	*Use Ryania*
phids		X	X								X	X	X
ean leaf beetles	X										X	X	X
utworms				X									
eafhoppers											X	X	X
lexican bean beetles	X										X	X	X
Vhiteflies											X	X	
nails and slugs					X								
phids		X	X								X	X	X
abbage maggots								X					
abbage worms; loopers	X									X	X		
utworms				X									
phids		X	X								X	X	X
abbage maggots								X					
abbage worms; loopers	X									X	X		
utworms				X									
arrot rust fly									X				
phid		X	X								X	X	X
abbage maggots								X					
abbage worms and loopers	X									X	X		

Vegetable	Symptoms
Corn	Silks missing; kernels eaten
	Tunnels in ears and stalks
	Plants eaten off at ground level at night
Cucumber	Clusters of small insects on leaves
	Whole plant eaten—vines and cucumbers
Eggplant	Plants stripped; (black striped beetle, red in larval stage)
	Clusters of small insects on leaves
	Clusters on underside of leaves
	Small round holes in leaves
Lettuce	Clusters of small insects on leaves
	Leaves eaten; earwigs present
	Edges of leaves turn brown; insects hopping when lettuce disturbed
	Leaves chewed; slime trails
Melons	Clusters of small insects on leaves
	Whole plant eaten—vine and fruit
Mustard	Clusters of small insects on leaves
	Leaves eaten by larvae
	Maggots on roots; plant doesn't look healthy

Pest	Hand remove	Water spray	Soap spray	Place collar around stem and into soil	Use beer containers	Put out rolled newspapers	Slit stem; destroy bug	Sprinkle wood ash around plant	Rotate crop	Use Thuricide	Use Pyrethrum	Use Rotenone	Use Ryania
Corn earworms	X												X
Corn borers	X												
Cutworms				X									
Aphids		X	X								X	X	X
Cucumber beetles	X										X	X	X
Colorado potato beetles	X										X	X	X
Aphid		X	X								X	X	X
Eggplant lacebugs												X	
Flea beetles												X	
Aphids		X	X								X	X	X
Earwigs						X							
Leafhoppers											X	X	X
Snails and slugs					X								
Aphids		X	X								X	X	X
Cucumber beetles	X										X	X	X
Aphids		X	X								X	X	X
Cabbage worms	X									X		X	
Root maggots								X					

Vegetable	Symptoms
Onions	Leaves wither; yellow insects at plant base
	Maggots on roots; plants don't look healthy
Peas	Clusters of small insects on leaves
	Holes in pods; blossoms eaten
Peppers	Clusters of small insects on leaves
	Plants stripped; orange and yellow beetles present
	Plants eaten off at ground level at night
	Tiny holes in leaves
	Leaves and fruit chewed
Radishes	Maggots on radishes; plants don't look healthy
Spinach	Clusters of small insects on leaves
	Tunnels through leaves
Squash	Clusters of small insects on leaves
	Whole plant eaten
	Plant wilts; flat, brown bugs
	Runners wilt; holes near base of stem
Strawberries	Fruit on ground eaten; slime trails
Sunflowers	Plant droops all of a sudden

Pest	*Hand remove*	*Water spray*	*Soap spray*	*Place collar around stem and into soil*	*Use beer containers*	*Put out rolled newspapers*	*Slit stem; destroy bug*	*Sprinkle wood ash around plant*	*Rotate crop*	*Use Thuricide*	*Use Pyrethrum*	*Use Rotenone*	*Use Ryania*
Onion thrips											X	X	X
Onion maggots								X					
Aphids		X	X								X	X	X
Weevils	X												
Aphids		X	X								X	X	X
Blister beetles	X										X	X	X
Cutworms				X									
Flea beetles											X	X	X
Pepper weevils	X												
Root maggots								X					
Aphids		X	X								X	X	X
Spinach leaf miners												X	
Aphids		X	X								X	X	X
Cucumber beetles	X										X	X	X
Squash bugs	X										X	X	X
Squash vine borer							X						
Slugs					X								
Stem borer							X						

Vegetable	Symptoms
Swiss chard	Clusters of small insects on leaves
Tomatoes	Clusters of small insects on leaves Plants eaten off at ground level Small round holes eaten in leaves Foliage stripped; large horned worm Small white insects flutter when plant is disturbed

Pest	Hand remove	Water spray	Soap spray	Place collar around stem and into soil	Use beer containers	Put out rolled newspapers	Slit stem; destroy bug	Sprinkle wood ash around plant	Rotate crop	Use Thuricide	Use Pyrethrum	Use Rotenone	Use Ryania
Aphids		X	X								X	X	X
Aphids		X	X								X	X	X
Cutworms				X									
Flea beetles											X	X	X
Tomato hornworm	X									X	X	X	
Whitefly											X	X	

garden, we chose the kind which had to be sprung from inside the tunnel—with the spring end fairly well out of reach. Though we have moles, we have not used mole traps, since those available here sit above ground and are very dangerous when activated. Those moles we have caught, we caught in the gopher traps—they aren't as effective, but we simply won't use the others.

If it gets down to the bottom line—safety is always first, and only you can determine what is or is not safe for your kids.

CHAPTER 6

Rainy Day Gardening—What to Do When You Can't Be Outdoors

Indoor gardening together is regrouping and learning.

It's the chance, first of all, to move away from the section, row and individual plant—the proverbial trees in the forest—to see your gardening from a different perspective. You and your child can take time to look at the *results* of his or her garden, however great or small. A part of rainy day gardening is decision making—deciding what to accomplish next year based on what happened in the garden this year.

Probably nowhere in your gardening experiences together will you and your child experience the dynamics of growth to the extent you do when gardening indoors. Hopefully, throughout the season, whether summer gardening or fall gardening, one of your goals has been to look for something new. Rainy day gardening is your opportunity to really dig in and examine what's going on—what growth is all about. Rainy day gardening is both overview and inner view. Each adds a dimension to your gardening experience.

We start our rainy day gardening at the fireside.

Plans and Superplans

Gardening results are part and parcel of gardening plans. Now that you've had a full year of gardening, experience—not just the advice of gardening neighbors, publications or your

Rainy days
are for planning,
repotting,
and taking a
closer look
at what
the garden,
however small,
offers.

nursery—can help you determine what next year's garden holds in store.

Serious gardening planning, the kind which produces really great gardens, begins with accurate record keeping. Sound dull? Or complicated? It's neither. I like the word "diary." Records are dull; diaries never. The difference? A human element—feelings and observations to go along with the facts. A garden diary is a total picture of your gardening experiences—the good weeks and the bad weeks, when such-and-such occurred and most important, why?

The types of things your child records about his garden should relate to his interests. Preschoolers, who, incidentally, will be intrigued with a garden "diary," will need your guidance in arranging pages and information. Keep things simple.

For our kids, the garden diary looks something like this. At the top of each page is a large picture of the vegetable we record on that page. Below, we print the name of the vegetable. In deciding what to enter we think of the garden in their terms—what was important to Johnny and Danielle as the season progressed? Several things come to mind. All basic.

What did we plant? How many days did it take to come up? What did it look like? How tall was it after a week? A month? What part of the plant did we eat? When did we first eat it? How did we fix it? Was it good? Are we going to plant it next year?

Older children will need information that can be applied to next year. Log information, leaving space for comments. In setting up a garden diary or record system, *purpose* is important. What will your child be using the information for?

Older children will probably have several purposes in mind. Competition might be one of them. In addition to general garden information, he or she will need to record which variety you planted and how it yielded—by weight, the largest fruit? The smallest? If you're in official competition, did you take a prize? If not, what did, and how did the prize winner differ from your entry? What do you plan to do differently next year?

In a cash-cropping diary, your child will need to know how much was spent on supplies; how the vegetable fared with its competition—was it early enough for a good price? Was it popular enough to sell well? Any complaints? What was the profit or loss?

Those are two examples of a specialized log. For the general garden record, you'll want to record some or all of the following: variety planted; how much; where you got the seed; dates of successive plantings; companion plants; how successful was the vegetable in terms of plant health, size, resistance to disease; yield; date to maturity; pest problems; when they occurred; how you treated the problem; special problems such as bolting, or failure to germinate; unusual weather conditions; problems you expected but didn't have.

Looking back, you'll have some idea why things happened as they did. Your child may have lost part of a vegetable crop to a late frost; tomatoes may have been exceptionally well-flavored and early because of your companion planting scheme and ideal weather.

From a record of your garden's year you can then project, and in some cases prepare for, what might happen in the season ahead. We know, for instance, there's a good chance we'll have an aphid problem next year because this year was exceptionally dry, and experts are predicting torrents next spring. Aphids are abundant after rain. However, ladybugs will be in short supply since many died from lack of food this year. Conclusion? We'll have to order ladybugs early and release more than usual.

Garden record keeping is not, and shouldn't be, the be-all and end-all of what happened and why. Some things simply won't be explained, no matter how carefully our child observes and records. But as a *guide* to garden successes and problems, psychologically they're valuable. If your child's tomatoes aren't all they should be, you can remind him that that late frost was felt by the farmer too. Then prove it by checking prices of tomatoes in the grocery store. You're still ahead.

In looking at garden yield, you can see where you overplanted and underplanted, then adjust next year's garden space accordingly. Now you and your child are ready to superplan next year's garden.

Garden Layouts

There's nothing wrong with a haphazard garden layout, if you have plenty of space. We've done it and it works fine. But if your area is limited, a well-organized garden will prevent some plants from being shaded by others, or getting more water than they should because of what's planted next to them.

Laying out the garden on paper reminds me of those puzzles we used to work as kids. You pushed the numbers around until they were in order, but to get one number positioned properly, you had to move five or six others. The same thing can happen in garden planning, unless you set some priorities. Through our mistakes we've learned more or less what should come first, then follow in order to have a workable pattern.

Back to ground zero, for the new year. We ask the kids what they want to grow, then decide on how much, using last year as a guide. (There's a limit to how much squash a family of four can eat.) Where we're going to put the garden is next. Then, working in companion planting, we place things on paper in relation to size—corn on the north side, with shade-tolerant cucumbers interspersed, for example. With the largest vegetables placed, we look at water requirements. There it is—tomatoes, a relatively tall plant requiring little water, will have to be moved away from the water-loving corn. That settled, we look to details. The squash we wish to use for next year's seed stock will have to be separated from the other squash plants to avoid the "crookneck pumpkin syndrome" we experienced this year. After we settle on a workable plan, it's time to compare with last year's. Carrots end up in the same place twice. We change that. Another quick switch and we have a better companion planting scheme worked out. From there it's the finishing touches—marigolds and nasturtiums in the nooks and crannies.

Fun Things to Learn About

You and your child have overviewed your garden success of the last year and have a basic garden plan for next year. It's time now for inner view, examination of the plant world in microcosm, beginning with life's package, the seed. Indoor gardening projects for fun and learning can be as numerous and active as your imaginations, interest in plants and the dynamics of growth. Right now, even if you haven't gardened inside before, you can start with seed and simple indoor growing projects, move to other forms of growing, then add houseplants as your child learns more about the special conditions of growth. You'll be well on your way to a lifelong hobby.

Seeds

Of course, your child will be quite familiar with seeds by now. Still, searching out different kinds of seeds around your home is fun for preschool children and points out that we could (and probably should) rely on the seed as a basic part of our diet. Start with the garage and you'll be apt to find bird or grass seed. From the kitchen cupboards there are sunflower seeds, possibly sesame seeds and the grains—rice, barley, whole wheat and rye, if you're into breadmaking seriously, then the seed derivatives—flour, rolled oats, cracked wheat and the legumes—peas and beans. Show your child the hidden seed "pits" of cherries, apricots or peaches. We liked topping off the seed hunt with a large coconut to show contrast in size and what seeds can taste like by the biteful. Finish your seed project by helping your child mount his collection and label it properly.

For your second seed project, get illustrated reference

books on trees and flowers common in your area. Plan a picnic in an unrestricted place late in fall and bring plenty of small sacks. Your kids can scour the area for seeds on the ground, in pods, in caches, on plants themselves. Sort them as nearly as you can (a magnifying glass helps). Sterilize good garden soil by heating it in the oven on cookie sheets at 180 degrees F. for thirty minutes. Plant several seeds of the same type in a small pot. The germination rate won't be nearly as good as your specially grown vegetable seed, but your child should have several weeds, wildflowers and maybe a tree or two come up. From there your detective work starts with the help of your books. By the time your child is through identifying his plants, he or she will have learned, first of all, to *observe* such characteristics as size, leaf shape, color, separate parts and rate of growth, and with your help be introduced to plant taxonomy. If you feel more secure with a back-up in case your child's seeds prove stubborn, send for some packages of wildflower seed mixes, which are available commercially. Plant them separately, but at the same time as your gathered seeds.

How Do Things Grow?

Even as adults, I think we all have those philosophical moments when we're struck by the power and mystery of life the tiny seed represents. I mean, who isn't impressed when, year after year, we scatter a handful of seed into the ground, and it comes up *at all,* then produces something we like to eat? That feeling is probably less profound, but even more real for our kids. Part of the mystery is that what a seed does takes place in the earth, where we can't see it.

This little experiment won't answer for your child *why* things grow, but it will give your son or daughter a good look at how.

Choose several types of large seeds like corn, beans or squash. You'll need several wide-mouth glass jars or drinking glasses, some blotters and a light, moisture-retaining material such as vermiculite, available from garden supply centers. Have your child cut a length of blotter to fit around the side of each jar. Insert blotter strips into the jars and half fill each with the medium. Add enough water to moisten the blotter. Next, have your child poke several seeds between the blotter and the glass. Set the jars on a sunny window sill and watch them over the next few days. Add water enough to keep the blotters moist, but avoid soaking the seed. In several days the seed coats will split, and his tiny plants will begin their travel upwards, just as they do in open ground. Little children are interested to know that a seed, no matter how small, is both the little plant and the food it needs to grow.

Producing Your Own Seed

While not strictly an indoor gardening project, culturing your own seed to produce varieties that do particularly well in your garden takes advance planning. Choosing the variety to plant in the first place should be done at the time you lay out your garden. Gathering seed you'll do just before the fall winds. Cleaning, sorting and testing must be done before spring planting, most easily, indoors.

The advantage of culturing your own seed is to choose the "very best of the best" you can grow in your area. A secondary benefit is that by growing your own you may not have to purchase seed next year, although you'll be investing your time. Third is the gratification you and your child will derive from producing a really good grower for your garden *from* your garden.

The principle behind growing vegetables for seed is simple—selecting good plant traits and, through successive years, producing better and better vegetables. To understand how selection works, you and your child can look up the basics of plant genetics, if he's interested. But make his garden the lab—that's where your child will learn the most.

To produce your own seed, plant only pure strains of the vegetable you select, since hybrids revert to the parent strains in seeding. Next comes observation throughout the gardening season. Watch each plant as it develops from seedling to mature vegetable. Be aware of a vegetable's most desirable characteristics—lettuce that is slow to bolt, radishes which are large, crisp, and firm, table tomatoes with tender skins and little core, and so on. As a general rule, if you'd really like to *eat* a particular vegetable, that's the one to save for next year's seed. Mark off those plants with string.

When the fruits are mature—usually after the time when you would normally harvest them for eating—pick the fruit, split it open and clean the seed. Soak the seeds of squash, cucumbers and similar vegetables in water to remove the pulp. Dry the seed on paper towels for several days, then store it dry, cool and covered, but not airtight.

For vegetables that produce seeds in pods, uproot the entire plant, hanging it upside down until the pods are brittle. Take care to uproot the plant before the pods shatter.

To test seed viability, soak a blotter and place about 30 seeds on top. Keep the blotter moist, but not wet, or the seed will mold before germinating. After germination, calculate the germination rate as a percentage. Knowing how much seed you have and how much you can expect to grow, based on your test, your child can plan how much to buy, if any.

In planting seed to produce your own, watch carefully for cross-pollination. Corn, cucumbers, melons, mustard, squash, onion, radishes and beets cross-pollinate easily. Some, such as beets and chard, will cross-pollinate with another vegetable entirely (remember our crookneck pumpkins). Plant these vegetables at least 100 feet from one another. Others which may cross-breed, but with less frequency, are tomatoes, eggplant, peppers and carrots. Beans, lettuce and peas you'll usually be safe with.

Rainy Day Growing Projects for Little Gardeners

Rainy day gardening with your child just begins with seeds. Your small child will be interested in other ways to make plants grow—without soil, in dishes and from kitchen discards.

The next time you serve garden carrots, save the ends. Trim the green tops to three inches. Fill a shallow container with water and stand the carrot up cut-side down. Place the dish in a window sill with plenty of indirect light. When the green shoots appear, move your child's water garden to the sun and the carrot plant will leaf.

As a companion to your child's water garden, make a dish garden in a similar manner, using half sand and half soil. Trim the green top of a beet to within a half-inch of the base. Next, slice the beet in two horizontally. Have your child plant the top section of his beet in sandy soil covering most of the beet. Place it in the light until shoots appear, then move the dish garden to a sunny window. Water frequently and your child's beet plant will flourish.

One rainy day gardening project your preschooler will particularly enjoy is raising a sweet potato vine. Take a large, deep water tumbler, a sweet potato, several toothpicks and some string. Help your child insert toothpicks around the potato about half way up. Place the sweet potato in water, supported by the toothpicks with the narrower end of the potato up. Put in a light window out of direct sunlight. In several weeks your child's potato will have produced a lush green vine he can train on a string around his window, making a unique "curtain."

Though it takes longer, an avocado tree can be lots of fun for your small child, and a special plant he can show his friends. Wash an avocado pit thoroughly, then insert three toothpicks into the pit for support. Rest the toothpicks on the edge of a tumbler filled with water, suspending the pit in the water. Be sure the pointed end of the seed is up. Place it in a warm, light window. When the "skin" cracks, peel it off and replace the seed in water. In several weeks, the seed will throw roots and split. Soon after, your child will be able to see his tiny tree through the crack. When it reaches seven or eight inches, cut back to six inches and it will branch. Help him plant his tree in good potting soil. (See houseplants, this chapter.)

Rainy Day Growing Project for Older Kids—Mushrooms

Considered a standby of the gourmet cook, the fresh mushroom is a challenge to grow and a delight to eat. Produced from spores instead of seed, and progressing through several unique growth stages in the absence of light, mushroom culture is an unusual winter gardening project well suited to an ambitious older child, who can even market his product if he chooses.

Mushrooms are fungi with very specific growth requirements. You and your child can grow them in several places—in dark or dimly lit spots in a cellar, under the house, in an outbuilding, under a greenhouse bench, or in a spring house—anywhere the temperature remains between 45 and 68 degrees F. for a period of three months or longer. The place you choose must be well ventilated and have a relative humidity of eighty to eighty-five percent. Your mushroom beds should be about six inches deep, not unlike flats, and are convenient to work with if you stack them in tiers.

A highly rich medium with lots of humus is ideal for mushrooms. Probably the best source we have locally is manure from stabled horses, which owners are very willing to let you shovel yourself. Mix this with fifty percent wheat straw, obtainable from a feed supply store. Mushroom soil must be composted at high temperature (180 degrees F.), then cooled to 70 degrees F. before planting. The most efficient means to compost properly is in a pile four feet by four feet by four feet, sprinkled with water and turned several times for proper aeration. When the temperature of the pile has cooled sufficiently, you're ready to fill your mushroom beds. Leave two inches unfilled at the top of the bed.

Mushroom spawn is available from many seed companies through their catalogs, and usually comes in "bricks." Your child should plant a piece of spawn the size of a walnut one inch deep, every ten inches throughout the bed. Keep bed watered with a light spray over the next several weeks. If the air is somewhat dry, cover the bed with burlap.

A week to two weeks after spawning, your mushroom bed should have produced its "mycelium," a network of threadlike filaments from which your mushrooms will emerge. The next step in mushroom culture is "casing" or spreading a one inch layer of good garden loam over the entire bed. (Peat moss can be substituted.)

Three or four weeks after casing, your child's first "flush" of mushrooms will appear. They can be harvested several weeks after as "buttons" or allowed to form flattened caps with the gills exposed. When harvesting mushrooms, your child should twist them off, then cut out the remaining portion of the stem, and fill with clean soil to prevent spread of disease from decaying stems.

From the time of the first flush, you can expect a crop of mushrooms weekly for the next few months, until the nutritional limits of the bed have been reached, or the weather warms up.

Houseplants Your Child Can Relate to

The houseplant craze has been strong for several years now, and no wonder, for houseplants bring the outdoors indoors in winter and add a dimension of coolness and serenity to a blazing summer.

Your child may already have received one or two houseplants as gifts, and if not in full appreciation of their aesthetic qualities, he or she probably enjoys tending them.

Growing plants indoors is experiencing, again in microcosm. Each plant has a life cycle and story of its own—particular qualities of shape, texture or color that makes it unique evidence of the diversity of all life.

Indoor horticulture will introduce your child to a controlled environment—a balance of light, temperature, humidity, water and plant nutrients, which determine whether or not plants thrive or fail.

The plants you select for your indoor gardening project should be chosen like your vegetables—with success in mind. In general, choose houseplants that are not difficult to grow under your particular indoor conditions. Beyond that, look for houseplants your son or daughter can relate to. So diverse is the indoor plant world that finding intriguing plants for your child, whatever his age, is the easy part. But first, let's take a look at what houseplants need to do well. Volumes have been written on houseplant technique, and you and your child will probably want to experiment with different growing conditions as your interest broadens. Here are the basics for getting started.

Potting Mixtures

A distinct problem of growing plants indoors is drainage (see chapter 7 on container gardening). One solution to this problem is to lighten the soil mixture, while retaining necessary nutrients. A mixture of two parts good garden loam, one part fine compost, one part coarse sand, and a sprinkling of bone meal will provide most of a plant's basic soil needs.

Temperature, Light and Humidity

In general, houseplants are comfortable if you're comfortable. Your child's plants will suffer in overheated, poorly ventilated rooms, likewise, near very cold glass or in drafts. Houseplants do best with some difference between nighttime and daytime temperatures. A five degree change in most cases is enough.

How much light a particular plant likes mirrors its natural habitat. Ferns, for example, being native forest dwellers, thrive in subdued light. Tropical plants tolerate more. In soft light, the brilliant color patterns of many broad leaf tropicals show green, reflecting the presence of larger amounts of chlorophyll. In stronger light, these same leaves may change to variegated reds—leaves with less chlorophyll.

All houseplants need a proper *combination* of temperature and light. Ferns require cool temperatures and filtered light; tropical plants, warmer temperatures and brighter light.

Humidity, the relative amount of water vapor in the air, is very important to plant health. Again, a plant's native habitat will give you a clue to how much humidity a plant requires. Ferns and tropical plants require a more moist environment than others, such as cacti.

Probably the most tricky part of growing houseplants successfully is finding the proper combination of temperature, light and humidity for each plant. How do you do it? Simply by moving plants around.

For instance, our small asparagus fern grew slowly but wouldn't have taken any prizes sitting on a northern exposure kitchen window sill, next to the refrigerator. We moved it to the bathroom and it has quadrupled in size and no longer turns yellow. The problem? Its spot in the kitchen was moist enough, but too hot due to the refrigerator air return. The northern light wasn't quite adequate. The bathroom, however, offered these advantages: high humidity, coolness (we close off that register very often) and filtered eastern light through frosted glass. We didn't have to create a special environment—it was already there. We just moved the ailing fern to it.

Water, Fertilizer and Houseplant Care

Once you've chosen your houseplants and found the best location, with water, fertilizer and freedom from pests, your child's plants should flourish.

In the beginning, we usually look up a plant's water requirements in a general book on houseplants, then adjust watering to how a plant seems to be doing. As with vegetables, when your child does water, it should be thoroughly, not just surface dampening. Some of his houseplants will do best if kept moist; others should be almost dry before watering again.

Fertilizing should be done regularly. We add bone meal to the original soil, then again when repotting. In between, every month or so, we fertilize with fish emulsion. You can also place a layer of compost, bone meal and wood ash (in small amounts) right on top of your pot. As your child waters his plants, the nutrients in this layer will leach downward towards the roots.

Your child's houseplants, when chosen with care and well tended, should thrive. Occasionally though, you may see an infestation of aphids, mealy bugs, mites, thrips or whitefly. The methods for pest control you use outdoors will work indoors as well. Control egg clusters and slight infestations with a water spray or a dilute soap solution applied to the plant leaves. Alcohol dabbed on egg clusters will destroy the most tenacious, but avoid touching the plant leaves with the mixture. For heavier invasions, pyrethrum or rotenone are effective.

To cut down on the possibility of pests, your child should quarantine new plants a week or so before bringing them near others. Sanitation is important too—remove all dead leaves from the bases of plants.

Houseplants Little Kids Can Relate to

Two types of houseplants your small child can relate to are those that move and plants that look like other things.

The Sensitive Plant

This plant has a gossamer look and a rudimentary nervous system. If touched or jarred, its leaves fold tight and its leaf stalk crumples. Several minutes undisturbed, and the sensitive plant resumes its normal position. Sensitive plants grow to a height of two feet with good care, but are not hearty.

The Telegraph Plant

A relative of the sensitive plant, the telegraph plant also droops when touched. In very hot weather its slender leaves oscillate, making the plant look as if it's fanning itself.

The Prayer Plant

Your child will find the prayer plant especially captivating since it moves *and* looks like something. Its paired leaf markings resemble rabbit tracks, so it's sometimes known by that name. At nightfall, its leaves fold, seemingly in prayer. The prayer plant is easy to grow, tolerates varying conditions, but prefers a humid environment.

The Spider Plant

A profusion of slender green and cream colored blades, the spider plant produces new plants on the ends of slender, elongated stems. The new plant clusters, with some imagination, do resemble spiders. This plant should be kept moist and in good light.

The Piggy-Back Plant

This one will do well on a window sill. It produces new plants at the stem base resembling parents carrying their young. The tiny plants can be removed and repotted.

The Umbrella Plant

Another indoor plant that looks like its name, the umbrella plant is easy to grow and can reach a height of two feet if kept warm, shaded and very moist.

Getting Started Houseplants for Older Children

The houseplants older children start with should be a collection of different looks and textures, yet be relatively foolproof. The following are popular for just those reasons:

The Boston Fern

The Boston fern, also known as a parlor fern, is one of the most lovely, spilling over the sides of containers usually hung from the ceiling. Like most ferns, it should be watered regularly, but never left soggy. Native to the forests, this fern likes cool air with high humidity. Your child can propagate it by dividing the clumps, or trying to grow new ones from the spores on the underside of the fern leaves. First remove the spores, spread them to dry for several days, then sow them thinly on fine soil. Dampen, cover with glass or plastic and put the spore bed in shade.

The Asparagus Fern

This fern is actually not a fern at all, but a member of the lily family. It's lacy and light, a deep forest green and easily grown. Like the Boston fern, it prefers filtered light, high humidity and cool temperatures. We give ours less water than the Boston fern.

The Bird's Nest Fern

For a larger fern, your child might like this one. It grows to a height of three feet, with sword shaped leaves.

Wandering Jews

Several types of houseplants bear this name. Wandering Jews have variegated leaves in browns and purples, pinks, golds and silvers. They're easy to grow in a variety of lights, preferring cooler temperatures and moist soil.

Coleus

The coleus is one of those plants whose leaf patterns change in response to light intensity. We have two growing under very different lights—one almost totally green with splotches of pink, the other purple and pink with green edges. Both were cut from the same plant. Your child will enjoy moving this plant around to watch the changes. Coleus cuttings root easily in water, tolerate strong light, and prefer moist soil. Pinch back the growth stems frequently to keep the plant bushy. You can find combinations in red, brown, purple, yellow, white and green.

Aluminum Plant

For the beginning indoor gardener, the aluminum plant is a good choice since it is easy to care for and grows rapidly. Its leaves are deep green with patterns of silver. A member of the nettle family, the aluminum plant should be placed in a well-lighted area and watered frequently.

The Gardenia

We've had extraordinary success with gardenias as a houseplants, though they're reputedly hard to grow indoors. They're well worth the risk for their reward of fragrant, pure white flowers. We started ours from cuttings rooted in water, then potted them like any other houseplant. During their period of active growth, gardenias prefer warm, humid conditions. Thus misting with water helps if your air is dry. Once flowering, gardenias need less water and cooler temperatures.

Episcia Cupreata (flame violet trailing plant)

For sheer beauty of foliage and contrast of color and texture, this is the houseplant your child should try. Its leaves are soft and fuzzy, copper colored with green veined leaves. Colorwise, the *E. cupreata* doesn't stop there—it throws runners and flame-colored flowers resembling tiny trumpets. Keep this plant shaded and relatively dry. The leaves are sensitive to touch and will turn brown if handled excessively. Avoid getting water on the leaves for the same reason.

Christmas Cactus

One of the forest cacti, the Christmas cactus has succulent looking stems that grow in "notches." They flower in profusions of salmon colored trumpets, nicely enough, in winter—thus their name. Be sure to plant this one in loose soil, more like the forests than the deserts.

CHAPTER 7

Special Gardens You'll Both Enjoy

Special gardens are like special people. They have a personality all their own and something unique to offer. A special garden should be your child's and your own creation—a place for wildlife, a miniature replica of your larger garden, a tiny sprout farm, a garden in containers, a science fiction show-off garden—and those you'll discover together. With special preparation, planning and good care, a special garden can be created indoors or out, as part of your larger garden or in a greenhouse.

Gardening with Wildlife

A successful organic garden is, among other things, a balanced garden. Part of that balance can be extending an open invitation to wildlife to inhabit your yard and garden area. We're blessed with more than our share of visitors to the yard now—toads, butterflies, chickadees, woodpeckers, quail, lizards, ground squirrels, gopher snakes, cottontails, jackrabbits and hummingbirds, to name a few. All these species of wildlife were there when we got here. Our job will be to preserve and add to the habitat we share with these creatures. That's a responsibility we take seriously.

Your backyard visitors are fun to watch, encouraging your child to learn about the larger scheme of nature to which

Some gardens have something special to offer: a unique plant, an indoor gardening experience, food for birds.

Man belongs. On the practical level, your backyard inhabitants are part of the bio-balance—a continuous food chain that benefits your garden by keeping pests under control, making fertilization thorough, and generally adding the health of your garden. The biggest part, of course, is the intense pleasure and the excitement in watching baby birds beginning to fly or your small pool attract the wild creatures you and your child may not have known lived nearby. In an ecological sense, when you garden with wildlife you and your child are instilling hope and taking one positive step towards preservation of a natural environment.

Before we get into the hows of attracting wildlife to your yard and garden, just what do I mean by wildlife? First of all, there are the birds—those native to your area, those that wing past your yard on migratory flights. The birds add color, song and life to your gardening space. They also devour numerous insects that otherwise might infest your vegetables causing damage. The common honeybee is another visitor who makes appearance from seemingly nowhere when the flowers you've provided come into bloom. They gather their nectar and fertilize your vegetable crops at the same time. With adequate water sources, amphibious wildlife will seek their refuge in your space. Frogs, toads and water snakes will take up residence, bringing with them appetites for the insects you wish to control and adding to the symphony of summer sounds at dusk. Depending on where you reside, larger animals—chipmunks, ground squirrels, rabbits, maybe even deer, can be invited to take abode. While some of these may find your child's vegetables tempting, a few precautions, like spreading blood meal to deter rabbits from the lettuce patch, will save your vegetables and encourage them towards the natural foods you've provided for the reward of watching their antics.

In thinking about inviting wildlife to your garden, though, you and your child must seriously look at expectations, then form your plan. If your lot is small, you can't hope to attract the number of wild creatures someone might who lives on several acres adjoining a wooded area. But there is a place in everyone's backyard for *some* wildlife. The chickadees and toads you attract will captivate your child as much as landing Canadian honkers excite someone with a backyard pond. Invite those creatures that are most likely to come.

Attracting wildlife to your yard is simple enough. If you and your child provide the life support your friends need, they will find their way. Food, shelter, protection from predators, and water are the major requirements—all easily supplied. For detailed instructions on specific types of wildlife and how to attract them to your yard, you and your child should check with the National Wildlife Federation (listed in appendix). In the meantime, these basics should give you a good start.

Begin by looking around your yard to determine what you already have that attracts birds, bees and other wildlife. If you have room to add to your landscape, think in terms of shelter and food. Trees and shrubs with berries provide both for birds. Next, take a look at water. Most of us don't have room for a pond, so use something much smaller. A birdbath placed in an open space visible from the air and where birds can be on the watch for predators will attract several different species. Lacking a birdbath, several large pie pans kept supplied with crystal clean water will serve the purpose. Remember that repeated visits can be encouraged by *steady* supplies.

Food is next on the list for birds, and if you don't have enough shrubbery to provide their needs year-round, you and your child can put food out. For summer feeding try seeds, grains and cereals. Craft books will give you several ideas on how to make bird feeders yourselves, or purchase them from garden supply centers or toy departments. In a pinch, try a shallow metal pie dish firmly anchored to a sturdy piece of lumber pounded into the ground. For winter feeding, birds need extra calories to compensate for the colder temperature.

Beef suet (fat) is ideal. Get it at little or no cost from the butcher. Hang lumps of suet from the limbs of trees in pieces of mesh netting. The birds can pick small pieces from the feeder, but won't be able to take off with the whole chunk. Good suet holders can be made from wood. Carve holes the size of fifty cent pieces at intervals along a piece of lumber or a log. Or simply nail bottlecaps along the length. Melt the suet at low heat, then pour into the holes and let cool. The log or piece of lumber can then be placed outdoors on a window ledge, or mounted on a stake, or fastened to a tree branch.

Another bird feeder can be made simply from pine cones. Tie a string around the pointed end of the pine cone to suspend it from a tree limb. Spread a mixture of peanut butter mixed half-and-half with cornmeal all over the cone. The small "shelves" of the pine cone hold the mixture very well, yet allow your birds easy access.

Note carefully, though, on winter feeding. Whatever you supply—seeds, grains, small pieces of dried fruit, peanut butter and cornmeal, suet—you and your child *must* continue to supply birds until natural food supplies become available in the summer. Birds feeding at your winter refuge are dependent on what you supply.

Flowers are another garden wildlife attractant. Flowers not only invite bees but butterflies, which in turn encourage birds to your yard. Amphibious wildlife will find its home in any fair-sized body of water—a small pool reasonably sheltered by low shrubbery. If there's room in your landscaping scheme, be sure to add a water source. With water and shelters of varying heights (tall, medium, small trees and berried shrubs) you need only add some additional food before your yard can become home for small mammals. Research with your child what those native to your area eat, then put out a supply—acorns, sunflower seeds, millet, nuts.

Planning your garden around wildlife is challenging and superbly rewarding. Some families have been so successful in providing refuge for wildlife, their yards have been certified as National Wildlife Federation Backyard Wildlife Habitats. Why not look into it?

Tom Thumb Vegetable Gardening

If you and your child haven't discovered the minivegetables, you're in for an exciting project and a real taste treat. Over the years, seed suppliers have developed midget vegetables which are exact replicas of the larger varieties. Tennis ball-sized lettuce, softball-sized cantaloupe and football-sized watermelons are some your small child will think are super. Add three-inch carrots, four-inch corn, four-inch cucumbers and walnut-sized tomatoes, and you can have a miniature copy of your larger garden, one even the tiniest child can relate to.

Minivegetables are a natural if you're hurry-up gardeners like us who can't wait to taste the "first fruits." Most mini varieties mature five to thirty days earlier than their regular-sized counterparts.

Minivegetables can be grown indoors or out, or in your larger garden. Since they require less space than regulars, they're a good suggestion for apartment dwellers who don't have loads of room. Many mini varieties do well in containers and can stay there the whole season. (Instructions are included below for growing minivegetables in containers. For more on container gardening, see Container Gardening, this chapter.) Like many regular varieties of vegetables, the minis do very well started in flats or pots inside, to be moved outdoors or transplanted, when the weather warms up.

Here are some to try.

Minicantaloupe

These little melons look like softballs and taste delicious.

Cantaloupes, like all melons, are a warm season crop. Plant indoors in flats or small pots. Cover seed a half-inch deep, no more, and press down firmly. Water thoroughly. When plants are well started and the weather warm, transplant into a garden area well worked with rotted manure. Minicantaloupes grow on running vines and require lots of water, so place them where they can spread, preferably near vegetables of similar water requirements. Top dress with manure several times during the season.

Cantaloupes are ripe when the rinds turn brownish and roughen, and the melon separates easily from the vine.

Containers: Use a tub and place outdoors where cantaloupe will receive at least four hours of sunlight. Avoid letting vines spread over asphalt or concrete, since the heat radiated from these surfaces might be too intense. If you can't let them run elsewhere, insulate with clean straw by placing it under the vines. This will also prevent rotting from condensation as the temperatures drop in the evening. You can also grow minicantaloupe on a fence, providing you support the fruit in a sling (use a nylon stocking tacked to the fence.) Fertilize with fish emulsion or a manure tea every three weeks. Check chapter 9 for fun eating ideas.

Minicabbage

Minicabbage is fun, to grow to show off to friends, and makes a nice single serving for a small eater.

Cabbage is a cool weather crop and should be grown early in spring or late in summer. It won't tolerate a hot climate. Plant seed a quarter-inch deep in flats or containers. Firm soil down and keep moist. Begin indoors about eight weeks before you're ready to set the plants out since cabbage is slow starting. Transplant to garden area, covering the plant right up to the bottom leaves. Let water soak the root area thoroughly after transplanting.

Minicabbage is ready to be picked when the heads are firm.

Containers: Minicabbages do well in planters.

Minicarrots

Even if your child hasn't been an enthusiastic carrot eater, he'll love these minis. The flavor of fresh garden carrots really make the case for growing your own, and minicarrots are even sweeter than regular varieties. My kids pull their carrots right up and eat them on the spot.

Carrots can be grown almost any time of the year, even though classified as a cool weather crop. Minivarieties need about 65 days to mature. Sow in rows, covering the tiny seed with a quarter inch of fine soil. Keep soil moist and green shoots will appear in about two weeks. Thin plants to two inches apart. Minicarrots don't require heavy feeding, so if your soil is already rich in organic nutrients, you shouldn't have to fertilize.

Containers: Choose a container in which your carrots can remain. A planter is ideal, or you can plant several to a pot. In planting, broadcast seed rather than planting in rows and thin as needed. See chapter 9 for serving ideas kids will love.

Minicorn

What garden would be complete without corn? None I know. And your child will think his mini garden isn't all there without popcorn, once you try these.

Minicorn is a warm season crop. It doesn't transplant well, but you can get a few days head start by soaking kernels for twelve hours before planting. Plant seed eight inches apart and cover with one inch of soil. Firm down. Keep moist and your seed will germinate in about ten days. Corn pollinates best near other stalks, so arrange corn in "blocks" rather than long rows. Stalks can be placed close together, since you can reach over the top of minicorn and your child, if he's small, can simply walk between the stalks.

Minicorn is a heavy feeder and will grow well in soil rich in leaf mold, compost and peat moss. Mulching helps too—a real bonus on scorchers like we have. Water frequently and consistently.

As soon as your minicorn tassles, your child can shake the tassles together to distribute more pollen to the silks. If you're planting more than one variety, though, place your blocks some distance from one another because corn is a cross-pollinator. If you plant "strawberry" corn next to Golden Midget, you're likely to end up with a red and yellow variety you won't be able to eat or pop!

Harvest corn for eating when the ears are full but before they turn starchy. Kernels should be juicy when you break one with a fingernail.

Popcorn is grown identically to other minicorn, except at harvest. Allow it to dry on the stalk. After ears are harvested, remove the husks and pile ears loosely in a cardboard box to finish drying. Shortly before you use your popcorn, strip the kernels from the cob and store them in a closed jar in the refrigerator. Kernels pop better if chilled.

Containers: Minicorn can be grown in a planter or in gallon cans, several placed together to form a block. Help your child hand-pollinate the silks. Keep well watered. See chapter 9 for fun things to do with your minicorn and how to pop.

Minicucumbers

Few vegetables smell and taste like summer so well as the cucumber, and the mini is no exception. Your child will probably make minicukes his project since they are easy to care for and lots of fun to hunt. Make great dill pickles too!

Cucumbers are a warm season crop that can be started indoors in flats or small containers. Plant about four inches apart and cover with a half inch of soil. Firm down and water well. When plants are well established, move to your garden area. Requirements of cucumbers are similar to those of melons—lots of water, sun and manure. Cucumbers grow on vines, so these minis will need some running room. You can place cucumbers either in rows or in groups called "hills." The main advantage of planting in hills is so you can fertilize several plants at once. Water often and consistently to prevent bitterness. Top dress with manure every few weeks.

Containers: Minicucumbers should be planted in a planter or a tub with precautions against hot cement or asphalt similar to melons.

Minilettuce

No garden would be complete without lettuce—to salad lovers in particular—and your Tom Thumb garden needn't be the exception. Minilettuce is no bigger than a tennis ball—perfect size for a one-person salad.

Lettuce is a cool weather crop that can tolerate some heat if planted in a semishady area. Sow seed indoors, scattering seed thinly a quarter inch deep in flats and cover with fine soil. Keep moist.

Seeds germinate in a week to ten days, depending on the temperature. When the seedlings are one and a half inches high and the ground is warm, transplant outdoors eight to ten inches apart in a well-fertilized garden area. Water well and consistently. Pick lettuce when heads are formed and still tender. If left too long, they will toughen and bolt (go to seed).

Containers: Minilettuce is perfect for planters, spaced ten inches apart.

Minipeas

These baby peas will really be a favorite if your child is small. Pods grow three and a half inches and contain peas the size of little pearls. You probably won't be able to feed the family, since it takes several pounds of pods to make enough servings for four, but your child should be able to grow enough for a special serving for himself. Your child will enjoy shelling the peas, a farm chore traditionally assigned to the youngest in yesteryear.

Minipeas are a cool season crop, so they will do well early in spring and late in summer. Plant directly into the ground or a container since they will not transplant. You can soak them ahead of time for faster germination. After inoculating the seeds, sow them one inch deep, about two inches apart. Cover, firm down, and water thoroughly. Tiny pea plants should appear in several days. Peas don't need to be fertilized, since as a legume they will restore valuable nitrogen to the soil where they are planted.

Pick minipeas when the pods are full and peas well formed, but still tender. Regular picking stimulates more flowers, so pick often and you and your child can enjoy several crops.

Containers: Minipeas do well in a planter or may be trellised along a fence.

Minitomatoes

If we had to pick *the* garden vegetable, I'm sure it would be the tomato (even if it is a fruit). Minitomatoes, sometimes known as "cherry" tomatoes, are sweet, fun to eat and mature well ahead of standard-sized models. The Small Fruited Collection, sold by Burgess Seed and Plant Company, will make a great show-off garden for your child. These tiny tomatoes come in two colors, yellow and red, and look just like cherries, pears and plums! Enough variety to make a special garden by themselves.

Minitomatoes are a warm weather, hardy crop. Like the larger size, they do require some tender loving care to get them off to a good start. Sow seed thinly and cover with a half inch of soil. Spray water gently over the seedbed and keep moist until seeds germinate in seven to ten days. Thin plants to three or four inches apart, unless you prefer to transplant seedlings first to pots, then to the ground. When plants are several inches high and the weather warm, transplant to full sun in a well-drained, fertile garden area. When transplanting, cover stems right up to the bottom set of leaves so they don't quite brush the ground. Roots form all along the stem underground, so planting this way promotes development of a good root system. Transplant after the heat of the day to avoid plant shock.

Tomatoes need lots of water but can be overwatered, especially when cared for by small children who think all watering is super. If your tomatoes are producing lush vines but few blossoms, and your soil isn't overly rich, cut back on water and they'll produce more flowers. In general, a good, thorough soaking every four days to one week should be sufficient, even in a hot climate. Tomatoes are heavy feeders and can benefit from a manure top dressing and mulch midseason.

Containers: Minitomatoes do well in planters, tubs or pots. They may be kept outdoors or indoors and fertilized with a manure tea every few weeks. Plants with small tomatoes still green on the vine can be brought in before the cold weather begins. If you place them in a sunny window, they will continue to ripen and flower—instant off-season garden!

Miniwatermelon

If you've decided against growing watermelon thus far because of the space they take, now is your child's chance without sacrificing half the refrigerator.

Miniwatermelons average three to ten pounds and come in several varieties—red and yellow fleshed and some with striped rinds.

You can plant and cultivate miniwatermelons just like minicantaloupes.

The most difficult part of raising watermelons is telling when they're ripe. The most popular way, of course, is to "thump" them. A practiced ear can recognize what's called a "dull" sound, every time. An easier way if you're not a talented thumper is to check the number of days to maturity in your seed catalog, wait, then try one.

Containers: Tubs work fine for miniwatermelons. Use a

heavy straw mulch over the soil to help retain water and give them plenty of it.

Sunshine Sprouts for Eating

Here's a garden absolutely tailor-made for kids—lots of fun, simple enough for any child and high in nutrition. What more could we ask?

Sprouts, familiar fare in Chinese-American cooking, up until several years ago weren't available in supermarkets, though they're a great addition to soups and salads. Recently they've grown in popularity and small wonder—they're the *taste* of spring mornings and freshly cut grass.

At first your child may not be too hep on eating them. But he'll love to grow them and offer the results for inclusion in the family menus. You can take it from there!

You can eat many sprouted seeds, including lentils, wheat and rye seed, alfalfa and mung beans. The latter are what we commonly know as bean sprouts. Alfalfa sprouts you've discovered if you like natural foods. They are what give crunch and flavor to the Sunshine Sandwich.

You can get seed for sprouting in any health food store, Chinese specialty store, sometimes your local supermarket. Or you can order seed from nurseries and mail order food suppliers. Be sure, though, wherever you get your seed, to use only that marked specifically for consumption. Garden seed, meant for planting, is often chemically treated.

Mung beans are a good choice for your child's first sprouting project. Have him rinse the beans (about a half cup) completely, then soak them overnight. In the morning, drain off the water and put damp seeds in a large wide-mouth jar. Cover with something water can drain through, such as cheesecloth or wire mesh. Put the jar in a cupboard. Several times a day, add water enough to swirl around, drain it off and replace the jar away from light (before school, after school and bedtime is fine). In three or four days, your child's mung beans will be bean sprouts of the Chinese variety and ready for eating.

For sunshine sprouts, start with a quarter cup of alfalfa seed. Soak them, drain and store in a dark place. Change water in the same manner. Your child's sunshine sprouts will be ready for eating in about seven days.

Container Gardening—Outdoors or Indoors

Gardening in containers is an excellent way to begin several kinds of special gardens—winter tomato gardens grown indoors, minivegetable gardens in small spaces indoors or out, controlled environment show-off gardens, or your child's houseplant collections.

Containers which will support plant life are everywhere, and some of the best are also the most common, like milk cartons, margarine tubs and egg cartons. To some special garden devotees, finding the right plant holder is a hobby in itself. The search for the right container—teacup or brandy snifter, sea shells, driftwood, brass kettles or milk jugs—takes parents and children from kitchen to seashore, flea market and beyond. One quick way to gather containers is to make a list of unusual ones and organize a neighborhood scavenger hunt.

While more difficult than gardening in the open ground, there are many good reasons for gardening in containers.

First of all, there's mobility. If your child wants to keep a little garden in his room for a while or take it to school, he can simply move it there. When the sun changes position during the year, plants can be relocated to advantage. You can switch plants from indoors to outdoors, stack them on shelves, or sling them in hangers—important if your space is limited and you love plants as we do. When a disease or pest infects a plant in one container, it can be removed from the others.

In a large garden, plants are affected by what is happening to their neighbors. For example, if you've discovered aphids and decide to remove them with a water spray, it will solve the problem nicely unless the vegetable under attack is in direct line with one that shouldn't be top-watered. When gardening in containers you don't have that problem. You can simply move the vegetable away.

You and your child can keep a close watch on growing conditions and very often solve a problem almost before it begins. If you're overwatering or underwatering, or if a particular pest has attacked your plant, the condition will be more obvious than in the larger garden where many things will be happening at once. Plants needing extra care will be easy to spot.

Another great thing about gardening in containers is that you are able to control, even create, special environments. Thus you and your child can have a variety of gardens—gardens in water, minature gardens, off-season gardens. The latter is one of our favorites. There's nothing like having ripe tomatoes on New Year's Day, and where we live, you can—with containers, indoors.

How to Garden in Containers

While gardening in containers is easy, it isn't entirely foolproof. As in your larger gardening projects, success depends largely on preparation and how you do things in the beginning. Regulating moisture is probably the most important.

Outside where plants and vegetables are unrestricted, roots can tap deeper to search out moisture. In containers, obviously, they can't. Soil that is too dry prevents a plant from getting water and with it, the nutrients it needs for growth. Natural mineral salts can burn plant leaf tips if not leached out by thorough watering. Good drainage is also a must. Waterlogged soil prevents air from reaching roots and stops beneficial bacterial action.

Pick containers with drainage holes or ones you can puncture. Punch milk cartons with a nail, tin cans around the base with a can opener. Small kids, it goes without saying, love to punch holes in things. With supervision, they can help.

The clay pot is an all-around container that is relatively inexpensive. Just cover the drainage holes with a broken piece of pot to prevent too much soil from washing away and plant.

Like many parents who wanted to container garden with the kids, we started following what seemed to be the simplest course. We dug up some soil, put it in the pot and planted. Our plants made a valiant effort, then died.

Too heavy a soil like clay will hold too much water as ours did, and your child's plants will suffocate; too sandy a soil will dry out. Ideally, your soil should be rich in organic material (humus) and plant nutrients, and loose enough to drain well. A formula that seems well suited to vegetables grown in containers consists of one part *good* garden soil, one part compost, one part peat moss and one part sand. (For houseplants, see chapter 6.)

If you have only a few containers to do, help your child do the mixing. If you have many containers to fill, make it a joint project—you can use a bucket or shovel and your small child a scoop or measuring cup. It will get the job done faster and will show your child proportion in action—it's not *size* that counts, but equal amounts. Mix your soil, scrub, soak, then fill your containers, and you're ready to plant.

Another consideration when gardening in containers is container size. Seashells, unless they're very large, are best for tiny plants; brass kettles for larger ones. If your child is beginning a plant from seed, start it in a small container. As it grows and its root system begins to expand, a container plant easily becomes rootbound. In general, transplant any plant to the next sized container. For example, if we've started in a two inch pot, we move next to a four inch pot, then to a six inch container. Some plants do best when slightly rootbound, however. A plant that continues to flourish should be left as is. Once growth begin to slow, that's the time for your child to repot.

Science Fiction Gardens

Plants have fired the imaginations of science fiction storytellers for decades—probably none so well as the carnivorous or meat-eating plants. Famous for luring and trapping insects for food, at the most, they may have something to say to grownups about man's place on this planet, if we care to speculate.

At the least, they make a really unusual addition to your garden and one your child will delight in showing his friends and taking care of as he would, say, a pet. Carnivorous plants are unusual, but also somewhat difficult to grow. They make worthy subjects for science fair projects for advanced child gardeners.

A carnivorous plant digests insects to make up for poor soil in its natural habitat. You won't need to plant them in rich soil or fertilize. If your plants are kept indoors, they may not be able to catch insect prey. Your child, though, can hunt insects for his "pets" with a butterfly net. These plants get some nourishment from photosynthesis as do other plants, and can store food for some time in their roots. If you really think they haven't had enough to eat, in a pinch, try a bit of raw hamburger.

Miniature Huntsman's Horn

This plant grows straight up from the ground in a stalk eight to ten inches high. At the top of the stalk is an opening which attracts insects. Sweet secretions inside the narrow stalk entice insects further and further down the stem until they are stuck, or fall into a pool of liquid at its base, thus meeting their demise.

Plant huntsman's horns in a container with a layer of sand below and sphagnum moss above. Sink the roots well into both layers. Huntsman's horns need lots of moisture and high humidity to produce their sticky fluids.

Hooded Pitchers

The hooded pitcher, like the huntsman's horn, rises above the soil in a stalk eight to ten inches in height. At the top is a "pitcher," an organ resembling a hood, and covered with translucent spots. Insects enter the mouth, which faces downward. Fooled by the light passing through the spots, they fly upward, hit the hood and fall into the liquid-filled stems, and thus to their end.

Pitcher plants should be planted root deep in sphagnum moss and watered frequently.

Cobra Lily

This plant bears a remarkable resemblance to the hooded cobra snake. Its long, forked tongue is covered with honey glands, attractive to unwitting insects who crawl inside the hood. The interior of the plant stem is lined with hairs pointed downward, which prevent the insect from crawling back to escape the digestive juices found at its base.

Plant cobra lilies in sphagnum moss and water frequently.

Butterworts

The butterwort is a low-growing plant with oval leaves that curve upward along the edges. The leaves are somewhat like flypaper—covered with tiny hairs and very sticky. The butterwort traps gnats and mosquitoes. In spring they bear violet or yellow flowers, shaped like tiny trumpets.

Plant in sphagnum moss, with adequate moisture, but not as much as other carnivorous plants. You can water, drain, then water again only when surface soil feels dry.

Adventures behind, adventures ahead. Your child's special garden is his alone. But there is a place for togetherness in gardening too. Your child can find this with other children in great group gardening.

CHAPTER 8

Great Group Gardening

Gardening in groups is fast becoming one of the most popular activities around. From tiny tots to retired persons, everybody, young, old and in between, finds pleasure in growing their own. Perhaps the pleasure people find in gardening together comes from feelings of solidarity—sharing work and sharing results, in short—community spirit.

If you're an adult who enjoys working with children, group gardening is your opportunity to teach and learn from kids. For kids, the experience will be more than just gardening. Interaction is as important as what is produced. Your child and friends will learn cooperation—how to organize for work, how to divide tasks, how to divide the spoils, how to find land and keep it. Working in large groups offers opportunities one-to-one gardening can't—chances for competition, even the opportunity to begin a business.

Funding Your Group Garden

Finding money for investment in seeds and garden equipment your first year will be a concern if your group is large and you don't want to foot the bill yourself. Depending on how much the group decides it will need, you have quite a few choices.

Members can each contribute towards the project by

Group gardening offers special challenges, but the rewards for both adult and child are special too.

membership dues from which purchases are made, or by contributing seed and tools directly. Your next source is what's free, such as tree leaves and other materials that can be hauled away, or what can be exchanged for group labor, like cleaning out stables. Check next for big bargains, like repairable nursery discards and packets of the previous season's seeds that retailers won't be able to market at anywhere near full price.

For equipment, there are several possible sources. Some city refuse disposal centers have a "thrift shop" where some types of salvageable equipment can be found. Somebody will have to check regularly since these items go fast. Direct donations are another source of equipment especially if your group qualifies as a charity, as many church clubs and youth groups do. Contact equipment rental supply houses and repair services. Rental outlets must replace tools frequently, and repair services have items customers haven't claimed. Businesses who donate can usually claim a tax write-off. Let everybody know what you need and you'll be surprised at what will turn up with very little effort.

When it looks like cash will be the solution to what your group hasn't been able to find, plan a fundraiser for "seed money" literally and figuratively. Try any of the standbys you think might work—lemonade stands, a flea market, bake sales, students-for-hire, car washes.

If these sources haven't met your needs, your group is probably large, and very likely affiliated—a scout troop, school organization, or something similar. Though it takes time and skill, looking for *project* funding can be challenging, and if you're lucky, rewarding—in cash.

Start with the community gardens. As mentioned before, many are already funded—equipment, land and seeds bought and paid for—and your access may be simply asking to join.

If your group is special in any way—handicapped children or the disadvantaged—contact related service agencies in your community. If funding for a project such as yours is available, they will know where. Adult service clubs interested in youth groups definitely shouldn't be overlooked. They are often project oriented and looking for groups to sponsor. Write to your local chamber of commerce for an organizations list.

Your school gardening group may be able to qualify for an actual budget through the science department or extracurricular activities; it never hurts to ask. Then there's sponsorship in exchange for advertising. A business may be willing to make a cash donation in exchange for advertising copy in your yearbook or school newspaper.

Any or all of these ideas are sources for beginning capital. You may be able to rely on some sources from year to year, like special project funding, the community garden or budget money. But probably you won't want to ask for too many donations from businesses, without making an effort to become self-sufficient. How to do it? Make your group garden pay. There's more about that later.

How to Organize Groups of Children

If planning is important for you and your child in your own garden, it's multiplied several fold when you work with groups of children. Unless you, as a group, can decide who will do what and when, group gardening just won't work. Success from the beginning is easy, though, if *everyone* knows what is expected.

First of all, what type of garden should your group grow? Summer gardens, without a doubt, are the most spectacular. But if your group meets during the school year, September through June, you have a problem. Hilmer Felton, a science teacher and gardening instructor for a California junior high school, has solved that problem, and others, nicely. His students plant winter gardens. The kids, he says, would always rather plant corn than potatoes. How does he deal with that? "First we take a look at germination times and length of time to maturity. The students know how long the school year is and how long a vegetable takes to mature. That's selective in itself. Next, we take a look at what's recommended. The students usually decide to stay with what's recommended since money for seed is limited, and they don't want to risk it on something that isn't likely to make it." He adds that they don't leave out summer crops entirely. The students who will be there to tend tomatoes, corn, and peppers may grow them, but the group as a whole focuses on cool weather crops primarily.

For a group garden to be really successful, the kids should make most of the decisions. Your role should be moderating rather than authoritative. To make sound decisions, your gardeners will need the proper information and know what's likely to happen in a certain situation. From there they should choose collectively—whether it's what to grow, where, how much, or specific rules for competition.

Which brings us to the second consideration in group gardening. Who is going to mind the garden when the group doesn't meet? When meeting with your kids for the first time, be sure this is resolved—by a volunteer, a rotating schedule, or your personal commitment to do it yourself. A whole garden can go bust for lack of water over one hot weekend.

Large groups of children can be organized into work crews, each with a team leader and assigned tasks. Let members choose their teammates and elect their leader, then define the bounds of his or her authority and responsibility. If for some reason you must assign leaders, pick the kids who seem to lead the others naturally. Later, whether you have assigned a leader or your crews have chosen their own, change around, so everyone gets a chance.

In any group project, there will always be somebody who is less cooperative than the others. Hilmer Felton formed his gardening class from children who were not model students.

What happened in the garden? There was horsing around for sure, he says, but the kids cooperate. In his gardening project, children must *earn* their right to be there—and they do.

Set your ground rules and stick by them. Felton's first rule is safety—infractions are not tolerated. For example, all students are given basic instruction in the proper use and maintenance of gasoline engines. Any student who doesn't adhere to the rules is forbidden to operate power equipment. Since rototilling is the most popular garden job, he says, he rarely has a careless student. He adds, though, that one student was eliminated from one group for "misdirecting his anger with a hoe in his hand." In certain instances, you can't afford second chances.

In your group gardening schedule, leave enough time for problem discussion. Hold regular meetings conducted by the participants, not adults, unless your children are very small. At your meetings, make team assignments, give the results of competition, garden project reports, or new information from study if one or two in the group have special interests they wish to pursue.

Take time to air gripes. Children have a well-developed sense of fairness, and should work out equitable solutions. For instance, in one garden group meeting a gardener complained that the boy working next to her always stepped on her onions while thinning his own. In this instance, the boy simply wasn't aware where he was putting his feet. Having it pointed out is sometimes all it takes.

Another child complained, so-and-so always walked through his corn. Others pointed that it wasn't marked and should have been. A fair solution to a fair problem.

Last of all, take advantage of your status as a group. Name yourselves. Felton's group receives a ten percent discount on everything purchased—seeds, hand tools, sprinklers, fertilizer, chicken wire, etc.—from three sources: a nursery, a hardware store and a wholesaler. Members should be alert for such bargains.

Finding Land Then Keeping It

Finding enough land for a group of children can be a problem. Basically, your sources are the same as those you would look to for a small family garden—vacant lots, government land, private owners. Once your group has a list of likely prospects, some member should present the project in a responsible manner. Outline your gardening plans making sure you've covered and presented solutions to any expected problems, like zoning ordinances.

Responsibility just begins with presenting a good plan for your group garden. Once someone has agreed to let your group use his land, each member is personally responsible for his or her personal acts, and those of the other members of the group as well.

One of your greatest allies can be those who live next to your garden—the neighbors. Each of your gardeners should befriend those living near, which means really making friends. After all, the neighbors probably weren't consulted on where your garden would go, and they have to live next to it twenty-four hours a day.

Befriending begins with sharing your gardening interests, and theirs, if they garden. Pass around what you produce, offer to till the neighbors' gardens while the group does its own. Everyone likes to help and your group may need some.

Hilmer Felton outlined just a few things their gardening neighbor has done for his group. "He's given us leaves for the compost bin, given us grapes in exchange for tilling his garden, lent us tools for one-time use, like his posthole digger. He's stuck his hose over the fence to water our garden if things begin to dry out, and often sets up his Rainbird for us." Felton adds that his neighbor has called the sheriff's office when someone climbed into the garden area heading for the tool shed. His role, according to Felton, doesn't end there. Their gardening neighbor is a resource person as well, willing to share his knowledge about plants and his skill as a carpenter. He's even given the kids snacks. "His mere presence," says Felton, "discourages vandalism and other problems." A neighbor who is a friend can be irreplaceable.

Dividing the Tasks—Dividing the Spoils

Nothing causes more problems in group activity, adult or child, than situations in which somebody always does more work than somebody else. For instance, one student in a city gardening project wore inappropriate clothing when his turn for working with the chicken manure came up. The first time, the others were understanding. He had activities after gardening, so he couldn't wear his old clothes. The second time, though, it didn't take the others long to find a solution. They scrounged up an old pair of sneakers and sweat pants for the errant gardener. Needless to say, he dressed appropriately from then on.

Sure, there are always those who willingly do more than their share, and that's fine. But you and your group must be alert to those who don't hold up their end. It doesn't hurt to remind everyone from time to time that each member has to earn a place in the garden group.

One good system for dividing tasks is the "job jar" approach. Make a list of what needs to be done in any week—thinning, weeding, caring for or repairing equipment, fencing, setting up an irrigation system, fertilizing, composting, finding lumber or composting materials, and so on. Each team leader picks a task. If some team prefers another job, bargaining is in order. If someone picks the same task twice in a short time, choose again. Or, you may find it convenient to make a master list of gardening tasks marked out by beginning, middle and end-of-season. Have groups draw lots for one-time jobs like building cold frames or rototilling. Continual jobs like seeding, thinning, weeding, watering, can be rotated to each team in turn. Team leaders should mark down who did what and when at the end of the day to avoid conflicts.

When harvest approaches, your group should work out equitable distribution of what's grown. Produce from the group work area is communal. What's grown in individual plots is sacrosanct. Here's where your good advance planning pays off. Hopefully, there will be enough of everybody's favorites for each. If not, the group should decide how to handle it—by drawing straws, bartering, or a "reward" system for work put in.

One sure-fire way to divide anything equally is to assign one or two persons to make equal piles. He who divides gets last pick. Piles under this system are *very* even. In general, how it's done isn't important. That there is agreement, is. Let the kids barter too—and encourage sharing.

Competition Group Gardening

Groups of kids gardening together means lots of vegetable variety. Everybody has the chance to grow his favorite—carrots, pumpkins, popcorn, watermelons, whatever.

Although certain vegetable varieties are especially chosen for competition growing, usually because of their size, like the larger pumpkins or beefsteak tomatoes, *every* vegetable is a likely candidate. Contests should be organized so there is a category for everybody and everything—the largest, the heaviest, the healthiest, the strangest, you name it. One local garden group looked up records of the largest vegetable of a particular type ever grown, then strived to beat it.

Judging should be impartial and, whenever possible, done by someone outside your group. Try a gardening neighbor or a gardening leader from another group. If that can't be arranged, group members can form panels and judge their own, provided all entries are "blind." No one should know who grew what until the decisions have been made. Be sure your group checks out local competition too—county and state fairs—and contests sponsored by gardening publications and garden clubs.

"Competition" will be forthcoming quite naturally, as children observe one another. One child will grow really great onions while another's will be puny. Here's the opportunity to encourage asking *why* so-and-so's grew larger. It may be that the first child spent much more time caring for his plants, that his soil was better or properly prepared, that he chose a variety especially recommended for the area. What a child learns from another in competition of this type, he or she is likely to remember—and apply.

Gardening for Fun and Profit

A well-organized garden group can produce much more than individual members can use. Your group can turn those perishables to profits in a number of ways to help fund next year's garden, and begin your group in the basics of business.

At the start of your gardening season, have group members check with retailers who might be interested in buying organically grown vegetables. Almost every city has at least one health food or organic food store. Go in person, ask what they need most, then decide if your group can supply. Don't put all your eggs in one basket, but if several retailers say they will buy a certain vegetable from your group, chances are, if you plant extra, you'll be able to sell it.

A fruit and vegetable stand owned and operated by the group is an excellent way to market your produce, providing you have a good location. If your garden is near a main thoroughfare, find out if you can set up right there. Just be sure to check into regulations and licensing. If you can't locate where the traffic normally flows, try an already established market where you can buy a stall for a small fee. Flea markets or local farmers' markets are likely places.

Don't forget the commercial packers or food processors, either. A group of children working in a local farming project sold their entire tomato crop to a nearby cannery.

One gardening project leader found a great market for what his kids grew. He checked with each student about his parents—what they do for a living and if they processed food at home. Such resourcefulness can result in interesting a grocery store manager-father in carrying your group's pumpkins, or pledges from several families for enough of a particular fruit or vegetable for their yearly canning.

If your group plans on them, special seasons like Thanksgiving, Halloween and Christmas are full of opportunities to turn your group garden to profit. Rainbow corn and gourds of all colors, shapes and sizes, are classic table decorations used in homes, by catering services, in restaurants during turkey season. Your first contact should be food service retailers, then gift shops, then individual homes, door-to-door.

The noble pumpkin *is* Halloween, of course, and your group can sell pumpkins by the pound from piles at your roadside stand, or right from the patch as pick-your-owns. Bake sales during the holiday season should feature fresh pumpkin pies, if some in your group enjoy baking. Again, don't forget the commercial canneries—canned pumpkin is a once-a-year item.

Christmas garden gifts are big. With imagination, creative packaging and reasonable prices you'll be able to sell many of the following: Miniature Christmas trees, started from seed in one-gallon cans. Rare or exotic plants started from seed. ("Exotic" is relative. What may be common in your part of the country may make a very unusual gift for someone's cousin who lives on the other side of the country. Or, order seeds not usually grown in your area, for gift items to give locally. See appendix for seed suppliers.) Gift items made from gourds, such as birdhouses and dippers, dried and shellacked. Houseplants started from cuttings, then supplied in decorative pots. Herbs, packaged individually, three to a pack, or blended together are also popular. No doubt your group will come up with many more ideas, once you begin to think in gift terms.

Giving garden gifts is only a tiny part of what to do with what you grow. The natural culmination of your activities takes place in the kitchen, where you prepare and enjoy what you've grown together. That's next.

CHAPTER 9

What to Do With What You Grow

I remember the first "serious" cooking I ever did. The casserole was a lively concoction of noodles, carrots, peas and onions in a creamy sauce; the recipe from a cookbook for children someone thoughtfully gave me for my birthday. Cooking the delicacy was a three-hour, rather messy operation. It *did* taste good when it finally reached the table. Hundreds of meals behind me, I smile, remembering Mom's patient guidance in what would today be a fifteen minute busy-schedule casserole. What Mom did was to introduce us—and there were five of us—early on to the proper preparation of good food.

The point of gardening organically, of course, is to grow good tasting, nutritious vegetables. You and your child start with organic soil building, progress through the year and end up, as we do, in the kitchen. Here is the culmination of your gardening activities.

The kitchen is your final proving ground. Success here is as important as success in the garden. That means knowing how to get the best food from your garden, how to prepare it. It means taking a look at kitchen safety, keeping things simple enough for your child's full participation, and finding recipes your child will look forward to eating.

The garden produce *looks* good, but the real point of organic gardening is in the eating. And in having your kids participate every step of the way.

How to Get the Best Vegetables from Your Garden

Organic or not, a vegetable picked past its prime won't taste good. In our garden, string beans are a case in point. The first year we greatly expanded our garden, the beans went unharvested too long. They toughened and swelled. Not wanting to waste, we prepared them anyhow, even froze some. After just a few bitefuls, the whole bunch ended up in the compost pile. A sad story, considering our gardening efforts, but we learned something. We have to check the garden frequently and plan meals in advance around our planting.

We try to avoid the frustration of overabundance—too many vegetables reaching their prime at once. It can happen if your child's garden is large, or if he or she has one in addition to a family garden. We've learned it's more satisfying to plant several small crops at intervals—succession planting—than going through the disappointment of having vegetables end up on the compost heap. Psychologically, being able to use most of the vegetables your child grows will add much to gardening success.

Hand-in-hand with good succession planting is timing harvests. Your child's vegetables should be young when picked. String beans are best with tender, unswelled pods, corn should be milky, not starchy, squashes tender (except winter squash), eggplant should be picked with skins still glossy, leafy vegetables like lettuce and chard, while the leaves are tender.

One of our local farmers always says, "Have the water boiling before you pick the corn." We weren't convinced there was truth in the adage until we tried it. Quick preparation, at least with corn, makes quite a taste difference. From harvest, we try to avoid any delay in preparation. We've also found that the "waterless" cooking method will preserve garden flavor and vitamin content in many vegetables.

Making Your Kitchen Safe

An alarmingly high percentage of all accidents occur in the home. Of these, accidents involving young children are most frequent in the late afternoon—the normal meal preparation and dinner hours.

Burns, cuts and falls are major concerns when kids are helping in the kitchen, most of all because little children are at a height disadvantage. For instance, to reach a mixing bowl on the sink, my daughter used to stand on a chair. Then one day she leaned over to reach something and slipped, cracking her jaw on the tile. To avoid future accidents, I try to bring the bowl to her level—mix things at the kitchen table where she can sit in her normal booster seat, which is secure. Cuts we avoid by simply remembering to place knives and other sharp utensils back from the sink edge, where they can't be reached by probing little fingers.

Burns are probably the most frightening. I know three children who have undergone plastic surgery or have it planned from identical accidents, which could have been prevented with a modicum of caution. Watch your saucepan handles. Keep them turned inward, towards the back of the stove. Children probably are warned not to touch something on the stove, but can easily run into an extended pan handle while playing in the kitchen. Charcoal cookers are the greatest danger outdoors. They can tip and spill hot coals causing severe burns.

Older children who are cooking should be taught how to light a gas appliance safely and how to extinguish a grease fire, should one break out. Instruct your child never to try to put out a grease fire with water. Flames should be doused liberally with baking soda. We keep some nearby always. As perfect as your garden tools, your kitchen implements must be in tiptop shape—no rusty knives or handles with splinters. Show your child the proper use of each utensil, and which to use for each kitchen task—paring, chopping, peeling, grinding, etc. All kitchen utensils should be cleaned and properly stored as soon as convenient after your cooking project. For everybody's peace of mind, insist on proper clean-up.

Simple Recipes for Young Gardeners

Julia Child notwithstanding, the key to good eating is often in simplicity of preparation. We all have favorite recipes that can be fixed quickly, with little fuss. It's been our experience with kids that they enjoy vegetables they can *recognize*, which are neither bland nor overly spiced. By all means, begin your kitchen fun together with family favorites.

Each year we try some new recipes for the vegetables we grow in the garden, but stick largely to the tried and true. Here are some our children like, which they can help fix and which they never fuss about eating. You're welcome to try them. (All recipes proportioned for a family of four.)

Snap Beans with Bacon

Whenever I serve this dish, Johnny used to say, "What did you do to the beans, Mom? They're *really* yummy." Now he knows, because he helps.

1 pound freshly picked snap beans
4 strips lean nitrate-free bacon
salt and pepper to taste

Wash the snap beans thoroughly, removing any stems and flowers. Snap the larger beans in two and place them in a one quart saucepan with one inch of water in the bottom of the pan. Add a quarter teaspoon of salt and bring the water to a boil. Reduce the heat and simmer gently until the beans are soft but not limp.

Fry or broil the bacon strips, drain off the excess fat, then cut them into bite-sized pieces. Drain the beans and stir in the bacon strips. Add salt and pepper to taste, then serve.

Lemon-Garlic Salad Beans

The rule of thumb around here is, if it has a little garlic in it, how can you go wrong? If your family has always used garlic, your children will probably like this recipe—especially on warm summer evenings.

1 pound freshly picked snap beans
¼ cup salad oil
juice of ½ large lemon
1 clove garlic pressed through a sieve
salt to taste

Wash the beans thoroughly, removing any stems and flowers. Snap the larger beans in two and place them in a one-quart saucepan with one inch of water in the bottom of the pan. Add a quarter teaspoon of salt and bring the water to a boil. Reduce the heat and simmer gently until beans are soft but not limp. Drain, and chill for three hours.

Mix the salad oil, lemon juice, garlic and salt. Pour the mixture over the beans and marinate for one hour. Serve chilled.

Squash Baked in Foil

If you've never eaten fresh pumpkin from the garden, you've got to try this recipe. The pumpkin tastes completely different from pumpkin pie filling; it has a delightful texture and a nutlike taste with just a hint of natural sweetness. Use this recipe with pumpkin or other winter squash. Kids can add the seasonings and wrap each piece by themselves.

1 medium-sized pumpkin, or 2 small winter squash
4 teaspoons butter
¼ teaspoon cinnamon
2 tablespoons honey

Wash the squashes and cut them in two horizontally or quarter them, depending on the size. Remove the pulp and seeds. (Save pumpkin seeds for roasting.) Place one teaspoon butter in the center of each squash piece. Drizzle the pieces evenly with honey. Sprinkle cinnamon evenly over the pieces. Wrap each in aluminum foil, sealing the edges carefully. Bake at 350 degrees F. until soft, about 45 minutes. Unwrap carefully (to avoid steam burns) and serve.

Summer Squash Parmesan

Summer squash can run you out of the garden, if you're not careful. The quantity you will have to plan around can be limited to an extent by picking the squash when it's very immature—about six inches long. Juicy and tender, our kids love squash fixed this way, but you must use small ones. Your kids can help chop vegetables and make the layers.

4 to 6 six-inch summer squash (zucchini is particularly good)
¼ cup fresh onion, finely chopped
2 tablespoons butter
¼ cup Parmesan grated cheese
salt and pepper to taste

Wash, then cut squash into one-half-inch slices. Place one layer of squash in a one quart saucepan with one inch of water. Sprinkle chopped onion, grated cheese, salt and pepper over the first layer, then add a pat of butter. Continue making layers until you've used all the squash. Bring to a boil, then simmer very slowly until squash is tender, about fifteen to twenty minutes. Serve hot.

Carrot-Raisin Salad

Occasions when a bagful of fresh carrots actually reaches the kitchen without having been eaten en route are a cause to celebrate at our house. This recipe, though simple, fits the occasion and is as popular as dessert.

6 medium garden carrots, scraped and grated
2 tablespoons mayonnaise
¼ cup raisins

Squeeze moisture from grated carrots, add mayonnaise and raisins. Mix thoroughly, adding more mayonnaise as needed. Chill and serve.

Eggplant Casserole

This meatless dish uses large quantities of the summer's most prolific vegetables—zucchini, tomatoes, eggplant and green peppers. Your children's help will be welcome peeling and slicing. We serve it at least once a week at the height of summer.

1½ cups cubed eggplant, peeled
1½ cups zucchini slices
1 cup ripe, peeled tomatoes, cored
2 medium bell peppers, sliced
1 medium onion, chopped
¼ cup salad oil or olive oil
2 cloves fresh garlic, peeled
salt and pepper to taste

Sauté garlic cloves in oil until brown, then remove. Add all other ingredients, cover and simmer for forty minutes on low heat. Stir occasionally. Remove cover and continue simmering for ten minutes, or until liquid has evaporated. Serve hot.

Swiss Chard Casserole

Swiss chard tastes somewhat like spinach, maybe a little stronger. It's best prepared immediately after picking. Even your smallest child can wash the leaves and tear them into pieces.

1 pound swiss chard
4 bacon strips
½ small onion, chopped
salt to taste

Wash and drain the chard, then tear it up, removing large veins. Place in a heavy saucepan with 1 tablespoon of water. Simmer until tender, about fifteen minutes. In the meantime, cut bacon into one-inch pieces. Sauté with onion on low heat until brown. Drain chard, then add bacon, onions and salt. Serve hot.

Vegetable Spaghetti

This vegetable is so versatile you'll be finding new sauces for it each year. My kids are impressed each and every time they pull spaghetti strands from what is obviously a squash. Use your favorite spaghetti sauce (everybody has one), or simply try this.

1 vegetable spaghetti squash
2 tablespoons butter
¼ cup grated cheese
salt and pepper to taste

Bake squash whole at 350 degrees F. for forty-five to sixty minutes, until squash is tender when pressed. Cut in two, remove seeds from center. With a fork, loosen spaghetti strands from rind. Place in warm bowl and add butter, salt and pepper and cheese—in layers. Serve hot.

Barbecued Garden Dinner— Shish Ke-bob With Roast Corn

Aside from the meat, your child's garden supplies the whole dinner. Kids love shish ke-bob and if supervised can pick, wash, chop, skewer and roast their own. What an accomplishment!

Marinade for Beef (for lamb, omit kitchen bouquet)

3 tablespoons kitchen bouquet
1 teaspoon salt
pepper to taste
1 clove garlic pressed

Shish Ke-bob

1½–2 pounds sirloin steak or lean lamb
4 small tomatoes, quartered
4 small bell peppers, halved
4 small onions, whole

Barbecued Corn

4 large ears garden corn
4 teaspoons butter
salt and pepper to taste

Prepare the marinade for the meat first. Cut meat into one and one-half to two inch chunks. Marinate for two hours, covered, at room temperature. Prepare the vegetables, then skewer, alternating meat, onions, tomatoes and peppers. (If your family prefers meat well done, add tomatoes to the end of skewer just before the meat is done to avoid overcooking). Barbecue over coals until the vegetables are tender and the meat is cooked to your preference. Turn frequently.

Corn should be husked, washed, then rubbed with soft butter. Add salt and pepper. Wrap securely in foil. Barbecue over coals, turning frequently, about fifteen minutes.

Popcorn

Older children can make their own; smaller children should watch Mom and Dad. Either way, popcorn is an ideal dessert or snack—especially in winter, particularly if your child has grown his or her own.

½ cup popcorn
1 tablespoon corn oil
¼ teaspoon salt
3 tablespoons melted butter

Preheat a heavy, four quart pan at high temperature. Add oil and popcorn, then cover immediately. Shake the pan quickly while the corn pops. When it stops popping, remove from heat. Put hot popcorn in a bowl, add salt and melted butter.

Minimelon with Ice Cream

Here's the world's fastest, and one of the best desserts. Use standard-sized melons or minicantaloupes.

4 minicantaloupes, cut in half, or
  1 large cantaloupe, quartered
4 scoops vanilla ice cream

Remove seeds and pulp from melons after cutting. Fill the melon centers with vanilla ice cream and serve very cold.

Stocking the Pantry

Teaching your children the art of food preservation while they are young will hold them in good stead in their lifetimes when, unfortunately, many predict underabundance, or its equivalent—high prices. But more immediate is the satisfaction and success of capturing your child's garden in pints and quarts that line the pantry shelves. It's a double delight—the best successes of both garden and kitchen.

To keep things simple, get organized before you begin processing your food. We assemble all needed equipment—utensils, jars, lids, rings, pans and ingredients. All equipment should be clean and in good working condition. Check all jars carefully for nicks or scratches and discard any that are not in good condition. Clean jars thoroughly in soapy water, then scald them either by pouring boiling water over them or running them through a hot dishwasher (150 degrees F.). Boil lids and rings in a covered pan to insure a good seal. Now you and your child are ready to begin food processing.

Strawberry Jam

Johnny helped with his first batch of strawberry jam when he was two. He picked the berries, then meticulously washed them, one by one. As young as he was, his greatest thrill was giving a jar of "his" jam to his best friend.

4½ cups prepared fruit (about 8 cups fully ripened whole strawberries)
1 package powdered fruit pectin
3½ cups mild-flavored honey

Gently wash strawberries in ice water. Drain. Hull, slice and crush 8 cups. Measure 4½ cups crushed fruit in very large saucepan. Add powdered pectin to fruit. Mix well. Place over high heat. Bring to a full boil, stirring constantly. Pour honey in all at once and stir well. Bring to a full rolling boil. Boil hard two minutes, stirring constantly. Remove from heat. Alternately stir and skim for five minutes to cool slightly and keep fruit from floating. Ladle quickly into prepared glasses. Cover jam at once with ⅛-inch of hot paraffin.

Dill Pickles

Summer wouldn't be summer without the garden cucumber, nor would picnics and lunches be the same without tingly, squeaky dills. September in our area is the ideal month to make enough pickles to last the year, or you can pickle a few quarts at a time through the summer. Kids are a big help with the scrubbing, the dill washing, the garlic peeling and the jar packing. They love the final product.

30 medium-sized pickling cucumbers
24 small-sized pickling cucumbers
3 quarts water
1 quart cider vinegar
1 cup salt
18 cloves garlic, peeled
3 teaspoons pickling spice
18 sprigs fresh dill

Scrub the cucumbers thoroughly with a stiff brush. (We scrub them twice, changing the water in between.) Mix water, vinegar and salt in a large pot, cover and bring to a boil. While this brine heats, add to the bottom of each jar three cloves of garlic and one-half teaspoon of pickling spice. Next, pack jars with cucumbers, larger ones first, tucking the smaller ones into spaces. Add three sprigs of dill, stuffing them between cucumbers so they don't float. Ladle the boiling brine over the cucumbers, making sure all cukes are covered and leaving one inch headroom. Wipe the top of the jars, place the lids and rings with a firm twist. Label and date the jars. Check for seal the next day, then store. Your pickles will be ready to eat in six weeks. (Note: We've never had a spoilage problem using this method, but you may wish to heat process pickles in a water bath canner.)

Roasted Seed Snacks

It's coincidental, but just this moment our largest crop of sunflower seeds is drying in the oven. The kids have been checking their progress steadily since last night, and if their enthusiasm is an indicator, they will have polished off the whole crop in two months. Better those snacks than what they're bombarded with on T.V. Supersimple this is!

sunflower seeds–5-10 large heads

Remove seeds from dried heads with a stiff wire brush. Spread on cookie sheets and place in sun to dry about two days, protected with wire screening. Or, oven dry at 150 degrees F. for twenty-four hours, stirring several times a day. Let seeds cool, then store in quart jars.

Pumpkin Seeds

Pumpkin seeds are a fun change from sunflower seeds, especially since you can't usually buy them in the grocery store.

Remove seeds from the pumpkin, separating them from the pulp as much as possible. Soak overnight in water to remove any remaining pulp. Blot on towels. Spread on cookie sheets and oven dry at 150 degrees F. for eighteen hours. Store in quart jars after cooling.

Peanuts

Dry roasted peanuts remind our family of the holidays, I suppose, because one of our favorite aunts always has a huge supply. With the kids growing them in the garden, we don't have to wait for the annual holiday trips anymore.

When your child's peanuts are fully cured, place nuts in shells on a cookie sheet and roast for thirty minutes at 300 degrees F. Turn frequently to avoid scorching. Let cool completely, then store in quart jars.

Peanut Butter

Homemade peanut butter has a lot going for it nutritionally. Lower roasting temperatures help preserve vitamins normally lost in commercial processing. You'll also avoid eating hydrogenated oils used in the national brands. To make your own, simply run peanuts through a meat grinder three to four times. When peanuts reach spreading consistency, spoon into a jar and store in a cool place.

Soybean Snacks

Dry roasted soybeans look similar to dry roasted peanuts and have the same "crunch" and nutlike flavor. Our kids eat them as eagerly as peanuts and sunflower seeds.

1 cup dried soybeans
3 cups water
2 teaspoons instant vegetable salt
1 teaspoon salt

Wash soybeans, add water and soak overnight in the refrigerator. In the morning, place soybeans and liquid over medium heat and bring to a boil. Reduce heat, add instant vegetable salt, then cover and simmer one hour. Drain soybeans thoroughly, then bake on a cookie sheet at 350 degrees F. for one hour. Sprinkle with salt, allow to cool, then store in quart jars.

A Family Gardening Album

These photographs of our family, but mostly of Johnny and Danielle, demonstrate to me what gardening with kids is all about. Both our kids are rambunctious and uncooperative at times, but almost never when they are in the garden. There's too much to do, too much to discover.

The photos in this album were taken by a free-lance photographer, Frank LaMoglia, who happens to be my father. It's only natural that his grandchildren should be among his favorite subjects, especially when they are at their best. And the gardening seems to bring out the best in us all.

The other photos in this book were taken by members of the Rodale Press photo department.

Johnny planting carrots.

Building the compost heap.

Johnny harvests beans.

Danielle and her daddy
plant a midseason crop.

)anielle waters her plot.

Johnny and I
check for cherries.

"Hey! Look at our radishes!"

Another load
of tomatoes leaves
the garden.

The end of a productive day.

Appendix

Reading List for Parents and Children

THE BASIC BOOK OF ORGANIC GARDENING
Robert Rodale, Editor
Ballantine Books
201 East 50th St.
New York, NY 10022

THE POSTAGE STAMP GARDEN BOOK
By Duane Newcomb
J. P. Tarcher, Inc.
9110 Sunset Blvd.
Los Angeles, CA 90069

GARDENING WITH WILDLIFE
National Wildlife Federation
1416 16th St. N.W.
Washington, D.C. 20036

Where to Write for Seed Catalogs

Burgess Seed and Plant Company
P.O. Box 3000
Galesburg, MI 49053

W. Atlee Burpee Company
Warminster, PA 18974

Earl May Seed and Nursery Company
Shenandoah, IA 51603

Farmer Seed and Nursery Company
Faribault, MN 55021

Henry Field Seed and Nursery Company
Shenandoah, IA 50602

Jackson and Perkins Company
Medford, OR 97501

George W. Park Seed Company, Inc.
P.O. Box 31
Greenwood, SC 29647

Seedway, Inc.
Hall, NY 14463

Stokes Seeds, Inc.
Box 548
Buffalo, NY 14240

Rare or Unusual Plants and Seeds

Armstrong Associates, Inc.
P.O. Box 94
Kennebunk, ME 04043

John Brundy's Rare Plant House
P.O. Box 1348
Cocoa Beach, FL 32931
(catalog $1)

Nichols Herbs and Rare Seeds
Nichols Garden Nursery
1190 North Pacific Highway
Albany, OR 97321

Suppliers of Predator Insects

Bio-Control Company
10180 Ladybird Drive
Auburn, CA 95603
(ladybugs, praying mantis eggs)

W. Atlee Burpee Company
P.O. Box 3000
Galesburg, MI 49053
(ladybugs)

California Green Lacewings, Inc.
2521 Webb Ave.
Alameda, CA 94501
(lacewing flies)

Fairfax Biological Laboratory
Clinton Corners, NY 12514
(lacewing flies)

Paul Harris
P.O. Box 1495
Marysville, CA 95901
(ladybugs)

Natural Pest Controls
1166 Bell St. Apt. 14
Sacramento, CA 95825
(ladybugs, praying mantis eggs)

Index